APOSTOLIC LEADERSHIP

The Bold Leadership
That Laid the Foundation of
God's Conquering Church!

Dr. Mosy Madugba

Copyright © 2018 Dr. Mosy Madugba

All rights reserved. No part of this book should be reproduced or transmitted in any form or by any means, electronic or mechanical, including photocopying, recording, or by any information storage and retrieval system without written permission from the publisher.

Unless otherwise stated, all Scripture quotations are taken from The New Kings James Version (NKJV) of the Bible.

From the publisher: Throughout this book, the feminine gender is seldom referred to directly. In the interest of simplicity, the author has used gender in the generic sense in most instances with no discrimination between the sexes intended. Apostolic leadership includes women of God.

In this book, the author, a master teacher, utilizes repetition to reinforce the major concepts.

7710-T Cherry Park Dr, Ste 224
Houston, TX 77095

ISBN: 978-0-9997837-1-9

Dedication

I dedicate this book to those apostolic leaders whose selfless labor of love has expanded the Kingdom of God, transformed lives, families, cities, nations, and mentored many Timothies and Tituses without strings attached. They are doing uncommon exploits around the world.

Acknowledgements

This book is the result of the efforts of my teachers, mentors, and leaders who invested their time, knowledge and friendship in me. I am grateful for the commitment of my family, staff, supporters, and for those who allowed me to learn how to lead with them.

Top among them is my wife, Chinyere Gloria Mosy Madugba, who is my reinforcement from heaven, and senior editor who plays numerous roles in my life. What can I do without you?

I am grateful for my late father Sir. John Madugba who created platforms for me to become a leader at a very young age. I am also thankful for uncle Dr. Dan Onwukwe who was the first to recommend me to Scripture Union (Nigeria) and to acknowledge me as a leader.

Thanks to the elders of Light Bearers Church who entrusted me with the challenging task of being their apostolic leader.

Thanks to my staff at the International Head Office and the God's Glory House staff. Thanks to the members of Ministers Prayer Network family and her leaders.

Thanks to Dr. Juergen Buhler, President of the International Christian Embassy in Jerusalem, Israel for believing in me, and giving me the opportunity to serve in different capacities in this global ministry.

Thanks to Eddie and Alice Smith, friends of my wife and me for almost three decades, who volunteered to publish this book in United States shortly after it was published in Nigeria.

And to my cooperative and understanding children—Michael, *the Commander*; Michelle, Dad's *Baby-girl*; and David, *the Monarch*. They have sacrificed some of their special time with me to allow me to do what I do. I will remain forever grateful to each of you.

Introduction

For years God has directed different people to encourage me to write a book on apostolic leadership.

I have read Acts of the Apostles in the Bible and several other books on apostolic ministry. However, I told myself I needed several years of practical experience in that position to be qualified to write on it.

In 1971 my father thrust me out into the mission field. Eleven years later I began pioneering spiritual and administrative leadership for people of different ages, and denominations for *Scripture Union* in Rivers State, Nigeria.

Ten years later I launched *Spiritual Life Outreach*, our ministry in Port Harcourt, Nigeria, which has provided the platform from which I started the *Ministers Prayer Network,* and other ministries.

I have been a student of apostolic leadership in the caring hands of the Holy Spirit and people who God has placed either over my life or across my path. The training has sometimes been torturous, full of twists and turns. Some of the experiences one wouldn't wish on their worst enemies, and some have been gloriously fulfilllling.

Presently, I provide apostolic covering and mentor-ship to over 2,000 leaders around the world. I mentor religious leaders, heads of states, governors, and mayors in the U.S., in Nigeria, and several other nations. Many have watched me from afar, and others followed me closely for several years before they finally requested my spiritual covering and mentorship. Each of them has helped me grow into my calling and offices.

I count it a rare privilege to be asked by God to write this book. I pray that it will bless you. May you catch the fire-baptism, the Holy

Spirit, the wisdom, faith, courage, and selflessness that equips apostles who lead the church around the world. To successfully pioneer anything, we must begin by becoming a godly person.

Commit yourself to acquire quality leadership and exceptional vocational life skills. Work to establish a good marriage (if you are married), to build a successful business, or to plant a vibrant ministry or church. Work hard, pray apostolic prayers, and carefully watch the company you keep. Read this entire book.

--Dr. Mosy Madugba

CONTENTS

Dedication i

Acknowledgements iii

Introduction v

Chapter One - THE APOSTOLIC 1

Chapter Two - WHAT IS LEADERSHIP? 31

Chapter Three - REVOLUTIONARY LEADERSHIP 41

Chapter Four - NEEDED: TRAINED AND TESTED LEADERS ... 49

Chapter Five - QUALITIES OF A COMPETENT LEADER 59

Chapter Six - THE MANDATES OF THE APOSTOLIC LEADER 95

Chapter Seven - LEADERS: ROLE MODELS AND MENTORS .. 123

Chapter Eight - THE CHALLENGES OF LEADERSHIP 135

Chapter One

THE APOSTOLIC

The word "apostolic" refers to a dimension of operation or lifestyle that reflects the characteristics of Jesus' twelve apostles and other apostolic people God has raised up in each generation since. An "apostle," whether man or woman, is one who understands and believes in a cause and is faithfully, and passionately committed to it. He is therefore empowered and commissioned to go and represent the sending authority to carry out specified assignments or to pioneer or trail-blaze the same cause. He is simply *one sent on a mission*.

An apostle is also a person who initiates a great moral reformation or who first advocates an important belief or system. The first 12 commissioned leaders with Jesus Christ were called apostles, but beyond them, we find others like St. Paul, the apostle. In some church-denominations or organizations today, the highest ecclesiastical officials are called "apostles." An apostle is a champion of a worthy cause. You will discover more about him as you read on.

Paul later explained that many others would be called to be apostles for as long as the church exists, we read in Ephesians 4:11.

"And He Himself gave some to be apostles, some prophets, some evangelists, and some pastors and teachers, for the equipping of the saints for the work of ministry, for the edifying of the body of Christ..."

Therefore, God has raised and still raises men and women to provide apostolic leadership. Apostolic leaders execute Kingdom projects, transform men and situations, inspire people to use their God-given potential to make positive an impact to affect generations. They are pacesetters for Kingdom lifestyle who leave unique footprints on the sands of time.

Such men and women carry apostolic anointing and grace. The apostolic anointing enables them to be proof-producers to manifest evidence of the power of God to their generation. It enables them to perform unusual miracles, signs, and wonders. They also carry a transforming grace that changes people's lives, their circumstances, and destinies.

The Holy Spirit empowers apostolic leaders today to live Kingdom lives and enables them to carry out Kingdom projects as He did in the ministry of the New Testament apostles. In Acts 4:33, we are told that it was with great power that they witnessed to the resurrection of the Lord Jesus and great grace was upon them all. Total reliance on and partnership with Him makes it possible to flow in the apostolic. He is our Mentor, Senior Partner, Helper, and Coach to carry out our Kingdom assignments.

Apostolic Highlights

Today, a fresh grace is being released to the Church to enable her to replicate and accomplish even more than they did; which will be required to bring our generation back to God. This grace is also necessary to empower divinely elected men and women to remove the fake building materials that were used either by careless workers or hirelings in the past and to rebuild, restructure, reinforce, and restore her glory. (1 Corinthians 3:10) Below are some noticeable traits we see in the lives of Jesus' early apostles, which the Church must key into to be restored to her rightful place.

Early apostles were born again

They were born again and filled with the Holy Spirit. Jesus testified that all their names were written in heaven. *"Nevertheless, do not rejoice in this, that the spirits are subject to you, but rather rejoice because your names are written in heaven"* (Luke 10:20).

Because they were born again, they could relate to and work with the Holy Spirit. *"That which is born of the flesh is flesh, and that which is born of the Spirit is spirit"* (John 3:6).

They spent quality time with Jesus.

They spent time with Christ and received adequate training in matters of the Kingdom. They listened to and watched Jesus demonstrate Kingdom principles, values, philosophy, and power. They learned as they watched Him pray apostolic, prophetic, warfare and breakthrough prayers.

They asked questions and received answers to their questions. They were involved in supervised fieldwork with observable results while Christ was with them. They made their mistakes, received His correction, and spiritually matured to be commissioned. They never admitted anyone into their inner circle who had not been through the same training. In Acts 1:21–26 we read:

> *"Therefore, of these men who have accompanied us all the time that the Lord Jesus went in and out among us, beginning from the baptism of John to that day when He was taken up from us, one of these must become a witness with us of His resurrection. And they proposed two: Joseph called Barsabas, who was surnamed Justus, and Matthias; And they prayed and said, "You O Lord, who knows the hearts of all show which of these two You have chosen to take part in this ministry and <u>apostleship</u>*

from which Judas by transgression fell, that he might go to his own place." And they cast their lots, and the lot fell on Matthias, and he was numbered with the eleven apostles."

Therefore, it is invalid for a new Christian to introduce himself as an apostle.

The Holy Spirit Has a Controlling Position

Apostolic leadership is unique because God initiates it. Man is only a yielded instrument playing that role.

In apostolic decision-making, the Holy Spirit always has the upper hand, even in the highest apostolic ruling body in Jerusalem in the early church. *"For it seemed good to the Holy Spirit* (first), *and to us* (second), *to lay upon you no greater burden than these necessary things that you abstain from things offered to idols..."* (Acts 15:28).

When Peter confronted Ananias and his wife Sapphira for lying, he rebuked them saying, *"Ananias, why has Satan filled your heart to lie to the Holy Spirit* (not to Peter) *and keep back part of the price of the land for yourself"* (Acts 5:3-4)?

How did Peter know the actual amount received from the sale of the land? The Holy Spirit must have revealed it to Him. We refer to that as a "word of knowledge," mentioned in 1 Corinthians 12:8. It is the ability to know something that cannot be known naturally. Had Peter not been given that revelation, he would have never known. So, the Holy Spirit's guidance is required for authentic apostolic leadership.

Apostolic, Earth-Quaking, Ground-Shaking Prayer

Prayer continues to be the spiritual "master key" that opens every shut door in the spirit. The apostles taught their followers to pray.

The New Testament Church was born, and the Holy Spirit first received at a prayer meeting in the upper room.

Intense prayer was the number one item on the early apostles' agenda. In Acts 6:4, we read where they pledged to give themselves continually to prayer and the ministry of the Word.

Here, in Acts 6:3-4, is what they said about the challenge of distraction by social services, in this case, their ministry to widows:

> *"Therefore brethren seek out from among you seven men of good reputation, full of the Holy Spirit and wisdom, whom we may appoint over this* [social] *business; but we will give ourselves continually to prayer..."*

The apostles were people of prayer. Apostolic prayers are powerful and impactful, Kingdom extending prayers that shake people, places, and things. We see an example of powerful prayer here in Acts 4.

> *"And when they had prayed, the place where they were assembled together was shaken, and they were all filled* [drunk] *with the Holy Spirit, and they spoke the Word of God with boldness"* (Acts 4:31).

The result was that they became intoxicated with the Holy Spirit and a new boldness, power, and unction came upon them all.

In Acts 12:5, when they had prayed, an angel came down and physically opened the iron gates. In Acts 16:25-39 we read of Paul and Silas, imprisoned in Philippi. They prayed apostolic prayers, and God sent a physical earthquake that destroyed their chains, their stocks, opened their cells, and set them and the other prisoners free. When the apostles prayed, infirmities were healed, and the dead were raised! (Acts 9:36-42)

Quick Answers to Prayers

God is anxious to manifest His agenda on the earth. The prayer momentum of the season we are in today will be stronger than it was ten years ago. God is answering prayers speedily when we call upon Him in spirit and in truth. As we give Him His rightful place, His presence will be tangibly felt in His Church. It's an exciting day in which we live. Prayers that ordinarily took a week, a month, or one year before God answered them, are receiving His immediate attention today.

When apostolic women prayed in Acts 12, the prison gates opened of their own accord. When Peter walked out of the prison gates, the angel took him to the praying people whose prayers had opened the gates for him. Apostolic grace makes one pray and sing in a way that shatters prison doors and breaks chains.

Simplicity

"Hollywood Christianity" that comes with showmanship, pomp, and pageantry will soon be obsolete. No longer will we be puffed up by the fact that we are spearheading massive ministries and experiencing uncommon miracles.

In fact, no room will be given at all to self and pride. True apostles will not be interested in the praise of men. Their focus will be entirely on pleasing the Master. They will take delight in raising disciples for the Lord.

Militancy

Apostles are militant. They take the battle to the gates of the enemy. Jesus said, *"the gates of hell will not prevail against her."* The Church will no longer be led by men, but by the Lord of Host, the Captain of heaven's armies, Jesus Christ, the Lord of Glory.

They will fight on their knees, and with the Word. They are not an organization or a movement. They are a special squad, the Lord recruits. It will be a Church that will identify what has hindered God's move and presence in His Church in time past and pay whatever price necessary to usher Him back to His sanctuary.

A warring Church will labor in prayer, for their converts, so that Christ might be formed in them and that they might stand perfect and complete in the will of God. (Colossians 4:12).

Mobility

The apostles are mobile people who readily answer "Macedonian calls" from near and far. Stagnant, dormant warriors are prohibited from being part of the army. Every warrior must be agile and mobile, continuously changing and moving. They will not wait aimlessly in the trenches. The fire on them will not allow them to sit idle. As they evangelize their Jerusalem, they also reach out to Judea, Samaria and the uttermost parts of the earth.

The apostles of old were always on the move, traversing many lands, conquering new territory. They were more interested in building men than structures. They took missionary trips to different places. As soon as they finished their God-given assignments, they'd advance to new territories. It was obvious to them that they had little time to accomplish much. They were not rolling stones. They did not engage in "hit and run" work. They were good finishers, completing a work before they departed to another place.

Strong and Hardworking

Apostles are strong and hardworking, not a sleeping and lazy bunch. They are given special strength from the Lord to soar high above the mountains and the billows of life. They do not succumb to weariness.

> *"Even the youths shall faint and be weary, and the young men shall utterly fall, but those who wait upon the Lord shall renew their strength: they shall mount up with wings as eagles, they shall run and not be weary, they shall work and not faint"* (Isaiah 40:30-31).

The apostolic Church is conscious of the fact that the harvest is plenteous, but the laborers are few. (Luke 10:2) She is also aware that God operates at jet speed, ready to take as many as can move with Him into the field. It is a season of quick work. God, is doing a lot of quick uncommon things today, and He needs men and women who are spiritually alert enough to understand the times and know how to accomplish their assigned tasks.

Unity

The apostles had all things in common. They had one focus, one mind, one faith, one united purpose and one God. (Ephesians 4:4-6) God's true apostolic Church, is a spiritual entity united in love, faith, fellowship, and ministry. It will not break ranks. It upholds all believers regardless of race, class, or color. Whether Jew or Greek, male or female, all are one.

According to 1 Corinthians 12:4-5, *"Now there are diversities of gifts, but the same Spirit. And there are differences of administrations, but the same Lord."*

Though we play different parts, we as one body are united in our diversity. The whole body cannot be an eye, or the head, or a leg. Each member has a role to play, for the benefit of the body. The unity of the Church is a spiritual reality. Although we have diverse ministries, gifts, and responsibilities, we are one in Christ.

We need to continually judge ourselves to ensure that our motives are pure. Pure motives will affect our mindset and our relationships. A united Church will be able to stand strong against the enemy and by so doing, ensure that God's agenda is carried out on the earth. The enemy can easily thwart the purposes of God if he discovers a divided Church.

New Testament apostles were the epitome of love and unity. The love they had for one another was unfeigned, genuine, pure, unconditional, uncommon, and uncorrupted. They did not minister for their own selfish purposes; nor were they like stagnant ponds that continually received but never flowed out to others. They were not the terminal points of God's blessings. They were channels of blessing. Blessings flowed to them and through them to others.

The Church today is multi-ethnic, multi-cultural, and multi-faceted. The walls of partition between us are being completely broken down. Soon, none shall say, "I am a Greek and not a Jew." Though our tribes, tongues, and cultures differ, our unity of heart and purpose will become foremost. The Church will not be established on denominational division.

Denominations will continue to exist for the purpose of identity, administration, and support, but the Church will not survive on a denominational platform. She will not be limited in her thinking and outlook by denominational doctrines. The Church will have a Kingdom mindset that can see beyond denominational distinctions to God's corporate Kingdom agenda. No matter how big a denomination is, it cannot stand in for a local church in the city, let alone for God's global Church.

Since we are all of one Kingdom, going to the same heaven, here on earth, we must receive the revelation of unity. There should be no room for segregation. Jesus had a dream team in mind as He prayed His last prayer on earth, *"That they may be one."* The church today will be the answer to His prayer.

More than anything, it is recorded in Acts 4:32 that the apostles had all things in common. No one claimed ownership of his possessions. They shared everything. No one had too much, and none lacked. Everyone's needs were met. This level of communal life will be ushered back into the Church in the days ahead.

Humility

The apostles learned humility. They were not born humble, but they chose to walk in humility. To humble oneself is a major responsibility of every leader, even more so an apostle. Humility, like a pill, should be swallowed daily.

To be a servant requires humility. Sadly, many leaders are unapproachable and unaccountable to anyone. Ministry flows from heaven through us to other people. If our ministry will be effective and minister life to people, we need grace. The era of ministers who like "bosses," lord over the flock is over. God isn't looking for superstars. He's looking for servant-leaders who will willingly lay down their lives for the flock; leaders who will not look for perfect people but, like David, will disciple a bunch of good-for-nothing fellows into a mighty army.

Preaching the Pure Gospel

The apostles redirected the world back to God's Word. In Acts 6:4 they said, *"We will give ourselves continually to prayer and to the ministry of the word."*

They did not preach entertaining massages. They preached sermons that convicted people of their sin. In response, those convicted asked, *"Men and brethren, what shall we do?"* Those early apostolic leaders were not intimidated by, nor did they fear anyone. As the Holy Spirit gave them utterance, they shared the full gospel without fear or favor. Thousands of souls were added to the Kingdom because of their preaching.

Their primary call was to see people saved and discipled. They often had opportunities to speak to kings and those in authority and conveyed clearly God's message concerning them. After Paul finished with King Agrippa in Acts Chapter 26, Agrippa admitted that Paul had almost convinced him to become a Christian. They never diluted their message to gain men's favor. They declared the whole counsel of God. In 1 Thessalonians 2:5, the Apostle Paul says,

"For neither at any time used we flattering words, as ye know, nor a cloak of covetousness: God is a witness:"

Some pastors today have lost this apostolic bold emphasis of preaching the pure Word of God. Some dare not preach it if it might offend the financiers of the church's building project. The new apostolic presence will address this and other related challenges that have bedeviled the church in the past.

The apostles had no time or interest in negotiating with the devil. They terrorized him at every turn. That is why the kingdom of darkness used every opportunity to blackmail them, or to see them removed from where God had placed them.

Demonstrations of the Power of God

Apostolic grace produces miracles. Peter and John boldly told a lame beggar in Acts 4:6, *"We do not have silver and gold but what we have; we give to you, in the name of Jesus, rise up and walk."*

The lame man thought they were mere religious, professional preachers. But when the apostles grabbed his hands, a power stronger than that of a high-tension wire surged forcefully into his body, straightening and strengthening his crippled legs to the point that he could not stand still. He jumped, leaped, danced and praised the Lord.

People leaving the beautiful temple hall that evening had Church outside. Wherever there is a display of the power of God, folks are ready to worship God. They want to stay anywhere God's power is demonstrated.

Dorcas died; they raised her to life. (Acts 9:36-41)

Eutychus fell from a second story window and died. But Paul said, "Not in my meeting." He went to the dead body and prayed him back to life. (Acts 20:9-10)

In Acts 19:11 it is recorded that *"God worked <u>unusual</u> miracles by the hands of Paul."* He startled his generation with unfamiliar demonstrations of God's miraculous grace. They were beyond miraculous. They were *unusual* miracles.

The apostles never followed signs and wonders, running from place to place to find out what was happening and where. Instead, signs and wonders followed them, and their preaching of God's pure Word. Many shall believe the gospel as they see the fantastic things that God will do in the coming days through the Church. Great signs and mighty deeds will be conspicuous. In 2 Corinthians 12:12, Paul testified to his converts that great signs and wonders were wrought through his ministry.

> *"Truly the signs of an apostle were accomplished among you with all perseverance, in signs and wonders and mighty deeds."*

Evangelism and Missions

Jesus clearly explained to the apostles their primary assignment in Acts 1:8

> *"But you shall receive power when the Holy Spirit has come upon you and you shall be witnesses to me both in Jerusalem and in all Judea and Samaria and to the ends of the earth."*

The central essence of the apostolic rebirth of the Church in the new season is to restore evangelism and missions to its original pivotal position. God sent His Son as a missionary to save the world. He did His job, and afterward, He established a missionary Church to finish the task. That is why in John 20:21, Jesus said: *"as the father has sent me, I also send you."*

In Matthew 28:19-20, He put it differently saying,

> *"All authority has been given to Me in heaven and on earth, go therefore and make disciples of all the nations..."*

The early apostolic Church took every word of these verses seriously. Evangelism and missions were central to everything they did. They and went about to implement them to the letter.

Because of this, God was happy with them and the Holy Spirit guided them. They turned the world *right side up*! They appeared before gatherings of national leaders, like a joint session of Congress, to be judged, threatened and jailed. But they even made good use of those opportunities to preach the gospel. And as they preached it, they healed people in prisons, on the streets, and anywhere they found them.

Some of today's pastors maintain their gathered congregations. They do their best to entertain and make them feel good, with a friendly, man-made gospel, to sustain the financial needs of their churches. Because the Church has stopped aggressive evangelism and missions, she is in decline in many areas.

Every hour, thousands of people step into eternity without Jesus. Satan seems to party every night as he counts his loot of souls who die without Christ. We must return to preaching and promoting world missions. Our church members need to hear us emphasize it every Sunday. Missions should have a prominent place in our yearly church budgets. If it is important enough for Christ to come and die for it, we should preach and promote it with our whole hearts. *This* is the essence of the apostolic grace.

Spiritual Warfare

The early apostolic company was a warring company. They confronted and conquered new territories with military precision. They taught and practiced spiritual warfare. A lot of the scriptural passages we use today in spiritual warfare training were given to us by those apostles. Below are a few:

> *"For we do not wrestle against flesh and blood, but against principalities, against powers, against the rulers of the darkness of this age, against spiritual hosts of wickedness in the heavenly places" (Ephesians 6:12).*

We can get even more if we begin reading from verse 10 up to verse 18.

In 2 Corinthians 10:3-6 we also read:

"For though we walk in the flesh, we do not war according to the flesh, for the weapons of our warfare are not carnal but mighty in God for pulling down strongholds..."

Paul was the warrior who trained the Ephesian Church in warfare. Because of this, they subdued the evil principality called *Diana of Ephesians*, that ruled the continent of Asia at that time.

The Church will be led by the apostles and prophets, to confront the menacing forces of darkness over cities, states, nations, and governments.

Peter explained in 1 Peter 5:8 that Satan *moves around like a roaring lion, seeking whom he would devour.* This means that not everyone is devour-able. Do not let anyone preach you into becoming a cheap meat for the devil.

All powers in heaven and earth have been given to Christ, and He has put the enemy's power under your feet. Have you ever read Luke 10:19?

*Behold, I give you the authority to trample on serpents and scorpions, and over all the power of the enemy, and **nothing** shall by **any means** hurt you.*

I recommend you read my book, *Four Levels of Spiritual Warfare*.

Kingdom Lifestyle

The current apostolic Church will not be a myopic (near-sighted) Church where people are interested only in carrying out their personal agendas. It will be a global Church, interested in recovering the nations of the world for Jesus and ensuring that the kingdoms of this world become the kingdoms of our God and of His Christ.

She will know the concerns on God's heart, and His primary concerns will become hers. Her satisfaction and happiness will be found in pleasing God. The first thing on her agenda is to see *the whole earth to be filled with the glory of God, as the waters cover the sea.* (Numbers 14:21) She will delight in making God happy and in allowing the Holy Spirit to supervise His Church as He desires.

They will not build for themselves, but for the Kingdom. They will lay aside their private agendas that would suffocate the work of the Kingdom. There will be more emphasis on interpersonal relationships than on personal ministries.

Kingdom priorities of the will supersede our different ministry names, which only distinguish us from each other. The Church in this will be trained to have a large Kingdom heart and to see things from a Kingdom perspective. Interpersonal relationships will be emphasized. The era of friends that stick more closely than brothers is now. The blood of Jesus shall be the binding force.

The Church will be obsessed with lifting up Jesus, so He can draw all men to Himself. (John 12:32) Christians will be preoccupied with studying and preaching the Word. The gospel must be taken to the ends of the earth.

God promises them His wisdom, guidance, and protection. They will not be exposed to the onslaughts of the enemy. For as long as they remain in His divine will, they have a sure word from the Lord that *no weapon fashioned against them will prosper. Any tongue that rises up in judgment against them will be condemned* (Isaiah 54:17).

The early apostles provided exemplary guidelines for Kingdom living. For example, they opposed racism and gender discrimination. In Galatians 3:26-29, they said there is no Jew, no Greek, no Gentile, no male, no female in Christ Jesus. We are all one. They lived and taught communal living. Acts 2:44 tells us that they shared everything they had. They were one big and ever-growing family, which is why their growth rate was phenomenal. In today's self-centered world we need to rediscover our apostolic role and practice it.

Ambassadorial Authority to Set Things In Order

The early apostles claimed to be ambassadors of the government of heaven. And as ambassadors, they enjoyed delegated authority, as well as spiritual and physical diplomatic immunity. (2 Corinthians 5:20)

The apostolic council of Jerusalem met regularly to pray over and discuss the welfare of the fledgling first century Church. In Acts 15, they met, discussed and as led by the Holy Spirit, gave direction to the New Testament Church.

In Paul's letter to Titus, in Titus 1:5 he wrote:

"For this reason, I left you in Crete, that you should set in order the things that are lacking, and appoint elders in every city as I commanded you."

True apostolic leaders provide biblical guidelines for the selection of church leaders, family life, and church government. They provide what is known as the church's apostolic doctrine. They clarify scriptural guidelines for Church discipline, and for ministry in general. Simply put, they set things in order. Wherever there is church confusion and strive, know that true apostolic leadership is likely lacking.

Boldness

They were bold and courageous. Boldness should be a major hallmark of the Church. Boldness has to do with refusing every form of intimidation, but being courageous, blunt, and outspoken. The courageous early apostles were not intimidated by threats or persecution.

> *"When they saw the boldness of Peter and John and perceived that they were uneducated and untrained men, they marveled. And they realized that they had been with Jesus"* (Acts 4:13).

One cannot walk with Jesus and be a coward. The Bible in Proverbs 28:1 enjoins us to be as bold as a lion. We must exhibit the boldness of the Lion of the tribe of Judah. We need boldness to carry out our Kingdom assignments. Some of those assignments may involve going to see men of high rank and authority, kings on their thrones. Others, confronting the gates of hell. We have no interest in negotiating with the devil. We have a mandate to root out sin, religiosity, and to pull down the strongholds of the enemy. We will not be dismayed or intimidated by Satan's threats. We are here to execute God's vengeance over His enemies and to pronounce His written judgments. Without boldness, we cannot carry out our assignments.

Notice that the apostles never asked God to stop their opposition. They understood that it was part of the package assigned to them. Consider the prayers they prayed in Acts 4:29 in the midst their persecution. *Their only desire was for more boldness to preach the*

Word, and God answered them. They knew their mandate was to obey God rather than men, and they were ready to lay down their lives for Christ. They boldly asked the religious leaders who threatened to kill them, to judge among themselves if it was not better for them to obey God rather than men.

When Paul stood before Agrippa, he defended God and his apostleship with boldness. By the time he finished addressing the king, Agrippa said, "Paul, you are beside yourself, your knowledge, learning, intelligence have made you mad. You almost persuaded me to be a Christian."

Paul was beaten one day. Blood gushed from everywhere as they finished beating him and led him to the gallery to lock him up. He said, "Excuse me, give me one minute." He turned to his brethren the Hebrews and began to speak to them in the Hebrew language. Ignoring his chains and his bloodied body, he boldly preached the gospel. Efforts were made to stop the apostles from preaching Christ. Though persecuted, they chose to obey God rather than men.

Absolute Dependence on Jehovah El-Shaddai

The Church in this era will learn absolute dependence on the Lord who will supply their every need according to His riches in glory. (Philippians 4:19) They will not depend on men; neither will they use gimmicks to raise money. They will understand that when God owns a work, He pays the bills. The Church will learn to consult the Heavenly Supplier when they run out of supplies because heaven's supplies never run low.

The Church must have confidence in God's provision. He desires to sponsor His work today. Our responsibility is to inform Him when we run out of supplies. The cattle on a thousand hills belong to Him. *The earth is the Lord's and the fullness thereof.* Distance cannot limit Him.

Teamwork

The Church in this era will work as a team. According to Ecclesiastes 4:9, *"Two are better than one for they shall have a reward for their labor... for when one is down, another will lift him up..."* A threefold cord cannot be easily broken. There are things that individuals may not be able to accomplish, things which will require a corporate anointing of two or more. A single tree doesn't make a forest. There will be no "lone rangers" in the Church. There is a reason why Jesus sent out His disciples two by two, and the Holy Spirit sent the apostles out two by two. (Acts 19:22)

This season is about a special army, under the command of Jesus our Captain, that cannot be intimidated by the devil. There is more emphasis given to networking in ministry. The body is made up of several interdependent parts: the hands, legs, eyes, mouth, etc. Each part will enrich the others. The body will be nourished by what every joint supplies. Ministry partnerships will be formed. God will cause the prayer Jesus prayed for His church to be one, to be answered. We will find strength through unity. Jesus worked with His disciples as a team and wants us to implement teamwork as well. We are not building our private empires, we are building His church.

More Training and Discipleship

The percentage of Church members today who are not disciples is alarming. But the Church in this era will become a training center, where converts will be prepared for spiritual warfare through prayer and the study of God's Word. Second Timothy 2:15 encourages us to *study to show ourselves approved unto God, a workman that needs not to be ashamed, rightly dividing the word of truth.* The Church is to be a military base where soldiers are trained to face the enemy and prevail against him at his gate. Adequate training will enable Christians to confront and subdue powers of darkness. The gates of hell will not prevail.

Jesus said in Matthew 16:18, *"and I also said to you that you are Peter and on this rock, I will build my church and the gates of hell shall not prevail against it."* We should note from this passage that Jesus, the Master Builder, the Architect, and Owner of the Church, will build her by Himself. As we partner with Him, He will build a strong militant Church against which the gates of hell shall not prevail.

Value will be given to mentoring as never before. Paul told Timothy in 2 Timothy 2:2, *"And the things that thou hast heard of me among many witnesses, the same commit thou to faithful men, who shall be able to teach others also."*

Fully Commissioned to Their Task

As Jesus commissioned the disciples before sending them out, so were the apostles commissioned by the Holy Spirit before they were released. The Church will also be commissioned by the Holy Spirit. The only secret to being able to fulfillll your commission is to be sent. Paul said, *"I have fought a good fight. I have finished my course, I have kept the faith"* (2 Timothy 4:7).

The apostles could accomplish their mission because they were sent. They were not only commissioned to preach the good news and make converts for the Lord, they were also responsible for perfecting the saints for ministry, developing leaders, confronting powers of darkness in the lives of people, and principalities over the territories they entered. They also ministered to the needs of their converts on various levels. These were not small assignments.

No wonder it was necessary that they were endued with power and authority before being sent. The power of the Holy Spirit provided everything they needed to succeed in their mission, ranging from the spiritual to the physical. Without it, they would not have been able to complete their task. They experienced His unction and refreshing as they carried out the work. It was evident that they were anointed.

Jesus has sent the Church today to fulfillll the Great Commission in Mark 16:15: *"Go ye into all the world and preach the gospel to every creature."*

Again, He said in John 20:21-22: *"Peace be unto you: as my Father hath sent me, even so, send I you. And when he had so said, he breathed on them, and said unto them, Receive ye the Holy Ghost."*

We need the level of anointing that the apostles had if we are to accomplish our assignments. The challenges facing us are no different from what they experienced. Prayer and the Word of God were the secrets to their anointing. Therefore, we must give these two their central place in the Church today.

A sent one is equipped with authority and power. Jesus sent His disciples two by two. Luke 10:1, *"After these things the Lord appointed other seventy also, and sent them two and two before his face into every city and place, whither He himself would come."* Before He sent them, He appointed them. Our callings are divine appointments, not man's assignments.

He also sent them out with a message. Anyone who must go for the Lord in this era must have a message given to him by the Lord. None shall be self-sent. They will be empowered to deal with demons and unclean spirits as in Luke 9:1, when Jesus called his twelve disciples together, and gave them power and authority over all devils, and to cure diseases.

Quicker Judgment of Sin

The apostles of old had no time to play games. They had the spirit of discernment and knew when their people were telling the truth and when they were lying. The case of Ananias and Sapphira in Acts 5:1 illustrates this fact.

Sapphira not only died because she lied like her husband. She also died because she was late to church. She arrived at the church three hours after her husband had died. Maybe she was busy dressing. Had she arrived on time, she would have witnessed the death of her husband who lied to the Holy Spirit. She would have told the truth and spared her life. But because she was late and did not know what had transpired before she came, she fell into the same trap. She told the same lie and died on the spot.

The apostolic church did not tolerate sin. Those who needed to be judged were judged instantly, and they died. There was no respect of persons. They were a noncompromising Church. Once you lied or deceived others, you were gone. If that were true today, I suspect that 75% of the people in churches will be buried in a week. The anointing to confront and judge wickedness is being returned to the Church today.

In Acts 8:18-22 when Simon the sorcerer, saw God's power flowing through the apostles, he offered them money if they would lay hands on him, and transfer their power to him. They said to him, *"Your money perish with you, you want to purchase the gift of God with money."*

Sadly today, some ministers who flow in the anointing, instruct their staffs not to allow anyone to see them because they are spending time with God. However, if you write a complimentary note on the back of your business card and attach it to a fat money-filled envelope, their policy will change instantly. They will come out like Gehazi, and say, "Oh blessed of the Lord..." Even if you are cursed by the Lord, you will be blessed, because your money has gone ahead of you. They will gladly prophecy empty words over you when the Lord has not said anything, so they can justify the contents of the envelope you gave them. May the Lord deliver us from such, in Jesus' name.

Building According to Pattern

The Apostles of old not only laid lasting foundations for their works but they also carefully built on them according to the pattern. Paul affirms this in 1 Corinthians 3:9-10:

> *"According to the grace of God which is given unto me, as a wise master builder, I have laid the foundation, and another buildeth thereon. But let every man take heed how he buildeth thereupon."*

God has expectations on how we should build, and the kind of materials we should use. As much as He needs more laborers in His vineyard, He is not careless about the pattern and materials they use. He clearly told Noah how to build the Ark. He also gave Moses the prescription for the tabernacle in the wilderness. He said to him, *"see that you make everything according to the pattern shown you on the mountain"* (Exodus 25:9). Even when Solomon was building the temple, God gave him every detail concerning the pattern and the materials with which he should build. God has not changed. He has blueprints for today's Church. He's not only calling laborers into His vineyard but insists that they build with the right materials, according to the pattern, so the edifice is not marred.

The Bible makes it clear in 1 Corinthians 3:13 that every man's work will be tested by fire. We may have worked hard for the Master, but if we have used the wrong materials to build, our works will be destroyed, and we will not be rewarded. So, the apostolic Church builds according to the pattern. Any work not built to His pattern is not His.

God, the Master Architect, draws the plans and supervises the work. We must build carefully and strictly accordingly. Anything done outside that will crumble. He's not only the Chief Architect, He's also the Estate Surveyor and the Master Builder. He is still giving models and patterns for His work today. His storehouse never runs out of materials, but many fail to consult Him before they build. Be careful how you build. He still demolishes buildings He has not ordained, or those not built according to His pattern.

Recognizing the Place of The Holy Spirit

The Apostles recognized the Holy Spirit and His rightful place in their work. It was obvious to them that the work was not theirs. The Owner of the work, the Holy Spirit, directed how it was to be done. He was not a mere after-thought. They recognized Him as their Senior Partner and Coach, without whom they could not do the work. They took instructions and directions from Him and allowed Him to pave the way for them, as they carried out their assignments. The apostles lived their lives in the spirit, not in the flesh. They had no interest in the works of the flesh. They were sold out to God and laid at His feet as a sacrifice. (2 Corinthians 1:4-10; 11:23-29) They knew that if any work was to count for eternity and pass the test of time, it had to be done in the Spirit.

Legislating for Heaven

They operated as diplomats of heaven, who could issue orders and make decrees on behalf of heaven. They were ambassadors for Christ. They not only made decrees, they enforced Kingdom conduct and holiness. Their voices were recognized in heaven and in hell. Hell trembled at the mention of their names. They confronted and intimidated the devil. They acted as God's spokesmen on earth. They often received and initiated new revelations God had for His people. They were the governing body in the Church to defend, direct, train, motivate, sustain, and guide her to her destiny. In Titus 1:5, we read:

> *"For this cause left I thee in Crete, that thou shouldest set in order the things that are wanting, and ordain elders in every city, as I had appointed thee."*

They were the heart, the centerpiece of the Church. They were indispensable. They set the tempo and tone for everything that happened in the Church.

They received impressive revelations from God but were careful not to be puffed up by them, or to use them for selfish advantage. Instead, they used them to enrich the Body of Christ, to teach them what the Spirit was saying to the churches.

If the Church does not know the mind of God, it will gradually become irrelevant to both God and humanity. Not everyone in the Church is able to receive God's revelations and explain them in a way that people will understand and run with the vision. Apostles fill this role in the Body of Christ.

Pioneers and Pace-setters

The Apostolic Church is a pioneering, pacesetting Church. Apostles initiate and push the Church forward. They keep her on the cutting edge and open to change. Any who resist change will stagnate. Those who will be relevant in this apostolic season must be trailblazers, pathfinders, forerunners, initiators, and "establishers." They will not only introduce new things, but they will launch the Church and guide her into her destiny.

Pioneers boldly break through seemingly impossible situations and open up nations to the gospel and to God's agenda for them. They penetrate areas others will have difficulty reaching. They usher in the light of the gospel, invade new territories, and engage powers of darkness there. They subdue them and bring those territories under the rulership of God.

It was the early apostles were change agents who set the standards for the Church. They not only knew the mind and purposes of God but executed them speedily. When God wanted to bring about a remarkable change in the New Testament Church, He introduced strong apostolic grace to facilitate it.

Integrity

The apostles were men of integrity who did not substitute charisma for character. They exemplified the values they preached. They lived blamelessly and worked tirelessly. They were not a burden to their followers and did not extort from them. They worked with their own hands for what they ate. Paul boldly asked his converts to imitate him: *"Wherefore I beseech you, be ye followers of me"* (1 Corinthians 4:16). If he were not a man of integrity, he would not have asked anyone to imitate him as he imitated Jesus. He took time to enumerate in his letters to Timothy what was, and still is, expected of anyone who desires to lead in the Body of Christ.

> *"A bishop then must be blameless, the husband of one wife, vigilant, sober, of good behavior, given to hospitality, apt to teach; Not given to wine, no striker, not greedy of filthy lucre; but patient, not a brawler, not covetous; One that ruleth well his own house, having his children in subjection with all gravity; (For if a man know not how to rule his own house, how shall he take care of the church of God?) Not a novice, lest being lifted up with pride he fall into the condemnation of the devil"* (1 Timothy 3:2-6).

Networking

Apostles have a special anointing to attract and network people in the Body of Christ. Other ministers submit to their authority. They motivate and mobilize God's army to fulfillll the Kingdom agenda. They know that to succeed, they must be able to disciple others to continue the work, or to enhance the speed of the work. They affect for good the lives of those who follow them, and they enable them to exercise the graces that God has placed in them.

Their followers are mature leaders, who believe in their apostolic mantles. They usher in the changes that should be found in the lives of individuals and the Church. They never operate alone but work hand in hand with prophets because through them they know the mind of God.

Paul's greatest joy emanated from seeing other ministers excel in their ministries to become all God wanted them to be. That was his motivation. He desired to bless others and sought ways to transform insignificant believers into great leaders who gladdened God's heart.

He did not entice people with material things to persuade them to join his apostolic network. People joined because they knew what they would gain spiritually and physically by submitting to his apostolic authority. When they felt like leaving the network, he released them without intimidation or harassment.

Optimism

The apostles of old had a positive view of life. Despite the challenges they faced, they rejoiced in their persecutions and held steadfastly to their confessions. For them, joy was not the absence of challenges, it was the presence of God. They sang and praised God in amidst their challenges. They lived one day at a time, not exchanging today's joys for tomorrow's troubles. Even in crises, they continued to praise and glorify the Lord.

They never saw the bigness of their problems or challenges, because they were focused on the bigness and uprightness of their God. They praised God even in the worst situations. Acts 2:47:

"Praising God and having favor with all the people. And the Lord added to the church daily such as should be saved."

In the same way, the apostolic church must be a positive thinking Church. She must allow the praise of God to be continually on her lips. God responds to situations based on how we see Him, and how we take Him in those situations. If we see Him as our great God, who is bigger than our challenges, He will be that for us. The apostolic Church should not think that the era of persecution and challenges is over. For she will enter the promise through trials and tribulations.

Focused

The work of the Master deserves our total concentration. It is important that we know our calling and God's mandate on our lives and refuse to be distracted. The apostles of old had a single vision and were bent on fulfilling it. Their priorities were ordered aright. They were conscious of the short time they had, and so accounted judicially for every moment each day.

To be an apostolic Church, we must be consistent, steadfast, and immovable. We must seriously dedicate ourselves to carrying out our Kingdom assignments. *"We must work the works of Him that sent us while it is day, for the night comes when no man can work"* (John 9:4).

Task and Relationship

The work is departmentalized in a way that no aspect of it suffers. As much as the real task of spreading the gospel and conquering new ground is given adequate attention, the welfare of the house should not be neglected. The apostles of old had all things in common. None lacked, and none had too much. Though from various tribes and tongues, with lots of cultural and economic differences, they were conscious of the fact that in Christ there is neither Jew nor Greek. They saw themselves as one in Christ.

They enjoyed unity in their diversity. Only unselfish, non-tribalistic people can achieve that level of unity. In this new move of God, He is linking apostles together from various tribes and tongues, across the continents. Though from different parts of the world they relate as members of the same family. They are concentrated on the Kingdom tasks entrusted to them while ensuring that no one is neglected in the Body.

Individual needs will receive attention. Every member of the Church will be valued. Those who need encouragement will be encouraged. Those who need to be physically, emotionally, or spiritually healed will be attended to. For Kingdom purposes, and to ensure that Kingdom needs are met, Christians will see themselves as stewards of what God has entrusted to them. In this Church, everyone's gifts and roles will be appreciated and used to serve the interest of the Kingdom.

Chapter Two

WHAT IS LEADERSHIP?

Leadership is the ability to inspire others to embrace a common vision, to accomplish the same task, and to achieve a collective goal. It is to see what others can't see, to recognize solutions, and to motivate the group to lay hold of them.

Leadership is not to acquire a title or to occupy an impressive position. It is to make such outstanding contributions in your field that people refer to you to obtain a clearer sense of direction, or to authenticate what they do. It is to draw the best out of others and inspire them to maximize their potential and to effectively use the resources they manage.

Leadership is an ability to inspire, encourage, influence, motivate and mobilize people. It is usually a combination of one's natural personality, knowledge and wisdom, skill and real-life experience.

There is a price to pay for one to become a leader. It is about *taking* the lead, not *"talking"* the lead. It's not about exercising authority *over* others. True leaders have followers they inspire, while authoritative leaders have subordinates over whom they rule. However, as has been said, anyone who claims to be a leader, and has no one following him is only taking a walk.

True leaders are trailblazers who set examples for others to follow and earn their followers through outstanding performance. Leaders are not born, they are recognized for their accomplishments in their field, which has nothing to do with race or color.

Leaders empower others to fulfill God's purposes for their lives, which involves helping people discover, develop, and use their latent gifts in the service of the Lord.

Godly leaders don't trust their natural abilities. Instead, they submit them to the Holy Spirit and allow Him to use them to bless others. They focus on their responsibility, not their authority. They fulfill their tasks with humility. God responds by authorizing them to lead.

Leaders not only share the organization's vision or goals with their followers, they provide the logistics required to accomplish the task. Good leaders inspire, motivate, direct, instruct, influence, and guide their people toward the accomplishment of their common objectives.

Leaders will often produce a sample of the product they want others to mass produce. It's leading by example, setting an example for others to follow. They blaze the trail and earn followers through outstanding performance. People are attracted to them not only because of their words but because of their accomplishments.

In Judges 7:17, Moses said to the people, *"... Look on me, and do likewise: and, behold, when I come to the outside of the camp, it shall be that, as I do, so shall ye do."*

A leader knows where he is going, how to get there, and what to do to take people with him. He not only has a vision of where his people are; he knows where they should be and how to make them uncomfortable enough where they are so they are hungry for the new place. He also has the charisma, grace, wisdom, patience and a tenacious spirit to persevere and bear with them, until they reach the destination.

Excellent leaders focus on their people, not merely on the task at hand. They use what power they possess as a tool for good, to bring healing to the hurting. They refrain from using power to frustrate, intimidate, or alienate those who oppose some of their views or approaches. Instead, they strive to teach and motivate others to fulfilll their destinies and maximize their potential, to be the best they can be for God.

For a leader to influence others to follow his lead, he must inspire confidence in them. He must earn their trust. It is easier for them to buy into the vision and run with it if they can trust you.

Good leaders identify the potential in others and help them use their potential for maximum impact. They are coaches, not commanders. Their higher goal is to raise other leaders.

Spiritual leaders strive to influence others to be more like Jesus to fulfilll His purposes. Their greatest joy is to see others reach their kingdom potential.

One should use his head to lead himself, and his heart to lead others. It's important to lead others with one's heart because they are moved by emotion. The stronger the relationship, the easier people are to lead.

To connect with people in a group, don't focus on the group. Relate to the members as individuals. It is the leader's responsibility to initiate connection. Good leaders give others credit. They talk *to*, not *down to* their followers. The proof of leadership is seen in the followers. When those you are leading are being lifted to greater heights and becoming better because of their association with you, then you are a great leader. They will, in turn, boost your potential as a leader.

Great leaders are change agents who turn bad situations around. They don't succumb to the norms or the status quo. They boldly challenge *what is* with *what should be and* lead the change.

We are not all the same, but we all have the capacity to lead in unique ways and at different levels. God has granted leadership skill to each of us in one measure or another. Seek Him, and He will reveal the guiding purpose and vision for your life and inspire you to fulfill it. By redemption, He declares that we are priests and kings according to Revelation 5:10:

> *"And hast made us unto our God kings and priests: and we shall reign on the earth."*

Prophetically we who are members of God's royal family, are endowed with excellence, which is an accomplishment, not an adornment. When we excel, like cream rising to the top, we emerge as leaders in our field. No one excels without paying the price, which includes reading, learning, and hard work.

Different Definitions of Leadership

The success or failure of any operation depends on its leadership. Several leaders have attempted to define leadership. Some people have rightly said that leadership is influence, but just influence is not enough. It has to be the right kind of influence. One can influence people to do evil. You could be very influential, yet not many people will want to hang with you over time.

Another school of thought views leadership as one who is headed somewhere with people following him. The problem with this is that when the so-called leader is lost, his followers are also lost. A confident leader moving in a wrong direction might well have enthusiastic followers behind him, but that if his team fails to succeed, he isn't a good leader. The real test of a leader is not where he starts, but where he ends up. The following are definitions of leadership given by some key leaders around the globe.

John C. Maxwell defines leadership as "influence and the ability to obtain followers.

Leadership is *influence,* nothing more, nothing less. It is dependent on someone catching a vision from God and mobilizing others to join them in its fulfillment. It is not about titles or positions or even functions. It's about *influence.* Your power of influence lies in your ability to get others to participate in your leadership. Influence is earned, not commanded. True leadership can't be awarded, appointed or assigned. Title can only buy you a little time to either increase your influence on people or erase it."

In his book *The 21 Irrefutable Laws of Leadership,* he also says:

"Leadership develops daily, not in a day. Leaders are learners, ever growing. To lead tomorrow, you must start learning today. Your leadership ability determines your level of effectiveness and the potential impact you can make on the people you are leading. Personal and organizational effectiveness is proportional to the strength of leadership. The higher you desire to climb in life, the more you need leadership, the greater the impact you want to make, the greater your influence needs to be."

John Maxwell believes that champions do not become champions in the ring, they are merely revealed there. If you want to be a leader, the good news is that you can. Everyone has the potential, but it isn't accomplished overnight. It requires perseverance, and you absolutely cannot ignore the law of process. Leadership does not develop in a day. It takes a lifetime.

He opines that it is not the size of the project that determines its acceptance, support, and success; it is the size of the leader. When it comes to leadership, you cannot take shortcuts no matter how long you have been leading people. To build trust, a leader must exemplify competence, connection, and character. Character makes trust possible, and trust makes leadership possible. We must trust one another. No man can climb beyond the limitation of his own character.

You earn the respect of your followers by making sound decisions, admitting your mistakes and putting what is best for them, and the organization, ahead of your own agendas. For John Maxwell, who you are dictates what you see. The more leadership ability a person has, the more quickly he recognizes leadership qualities or a lack of them in others. The better leader you are, the better leaders you will attract. If you think your people are negative, then you better check your attitude.

Maxwell believes that people first buy into the leader before they buy into the vision. The leader finds the dreams and then the people, but the people find the leader then the dream. People do not, at first, follow-worthy causes; they follow-worthy leaders, who promote worthwhile causes. People want to go along with people they will get along with.

People cannot give away what they do not possess. Followers simply cannot develop leaders. Only a leader can raise up leaders. In Maxwell's opinion, when the pressure is on, great leaders are at their best, whatever is inside them will surface. Leaders who practice the law of victory have no "Plan B," which keeps them fighting. Victorious leaders feel the alternative to winning (losing) is unacceptable, so they figure out how to achieve victory, and then they go after it with everything at their disposal.

Only a leader can create momentum which followers will catch. When a leader has the momentum, the future looks bright, obstacles appear small, and trouble seems temporary. To create momentum, one must be able to motivate others, and not wait to be motivated. Incredible things happen when the right leader and the right timing come together. The people's capacity to achieve is determined by their leader's ability to empower them. A true leader will always find a way to make things happen. To become indispensable is to make yourself dispensable. The law of sacrifice says you have to give up, to go up. Sacrifice is an ongoing process, not a one-time payment. It's a lifestyle.

John Haggai in his book *Lead On* defines leadership as "the discipline of deliberately exerting special influence within a group to move it toward achieving goals of beneficial permanence, that fulfilll the group's real needs." This definition suggests that leaders must consciously carry out this task and have the discipline to do it before it is done. They must commit to this task. One's followers need to be happy and satisfied with the spirit of unity and cooperation to pursue and complete the tasks.

Rev. Dr. Umah Ukpai, one of Africa's most outstanding and successful evangelists, defines leadership as "the art of influencing and directing men in such a way as to obtain their obedience, confidence, respect, and loyal cooperation to accomplish the mission of the organization. A good leader understands his tasks, knows his strengths and weaknesses, and is able to use them well to accomplish his goals."

Durbin Andrew defines leadership as "the ability to inspire confidence and support among the people who are needed to achieve organizational goals. Leaders must be able to encourage and inspire their followers to achieve the goals of the organization or ministry. They should motivate and coordinate their people to achieve their set goals. They should not only share visions but provide the direction and strategy to accomplish the vision."

Oswald Sanders in his book *Spiritual Leadership* defines leadership "as influence, as the ability of one person to influence others to follow his or her lead. He opined that every good leader is primarily concerned with the well-being of his people. He provides the needed guidance to enable his followers fulfill their assignment."

Quotes by great leaders in different fields

"A leader is the one who climbs the tallest tree, surveys the entire situation and yells, 'Wrong jungle!'" –*Stephen Covey*

"Leadership means setting an example. When you find yourself in a position of leadership, people follow your every move. " –*Lee Iacocca*

"You have achieved excellence as a leader when people will follow you everywhere, even if it is only out of curiosity." –*Colin Powell*

"The real leader holds the power, not just the position. Being in power is like being a lady. If you must tell people you are there, then you aren't." –*Margaret Thatcher*

"The secret of success in life is for a man to be ready for his time when it comes." –*Benjamin Disraeli*

"A leader is one who sees more than others see, and sees before others do." –*Leroy Eims*

"When you become a leader, you lose the right to think about yourself." –*Gerald Brooks*

"Leadership is one of the things you cannot delegate. You either exercise it or abdicate it." –*Robert Goizmeta*

Apostolic Leadership

Apostolic leadership is selfless leadership provided through a total dependence on the Holy Spirit. It is characterized by outstanding wisdom and knowledge of the Word of God, pioneering abilities, holiness, humility, honesty, hard-work, passionate faith-prayers, courage, unwavering faith, and strong confidence in God and His Word. It provides necessary supernatural demonstrations of God's power when needed to jump-start or pioneer a cause or project to completion.

Chapter Three

REVOLUTIONARY LEADERSHIP

Jesus laid the foundation of the revolutionary paradox called *servant-leadership* and explained the concept in Mark 10:42-45.

> *"Jesus called them together and said, 'You know that those who are regarded as rulers of the Gentiles lord it over them, and their high officials exercise authority over them. Not so with you. Instead, whoever wants to become great among you must be your servant, and whoever wants to be first must be slave of all. For even the Son of Man did not come to be served, but to serve, and to give his life as a ransom for many."*

Jesus taught an approach to leadership which did not exist until He taught it to His disciples. It is revolutionary. It's God's Kingdom type of leadership. He is the perfect example of a servant-leader. Our study on servant-leadership would be incomplete without referring to Him.

Christ led by example. While other leaders waited to be served, He stooped and washed the feet of His disciples who were supposed to be His servants. That is the demeaning work a leader can do for his followers. But Jesus did it to reveal a new Kingdom pattern of leadership we call, *servant-leadership*.

Servant-Leadership

Servant-leaders empower others through selfless love to discover and to fulfil their gifts and purposes in life; then to lovingly help deploy them into the service of the Lord and humanity.

Servant-leaders don't focus on securing positions at the detriment of people. A servant-leader views power as a righteous instrument for doing good and bringing healing to the hurting. He refrains from intentionally using his power to frustrate, intimidate, or alienate those who are opposed to some of his views or approaches. He strives to build bridges of loving relationships among those under his oversight. A servant-leader uses his time, money, gift and his life to serve God and God's people, following the example of his Master (Jesus Christ), who laid down his life for the sheep.

A servant-leader builds and equips believers for effective service in the Lord's vineyard; essentially harnessing and organizing them to maximize their productivity. The leader mobilizes, inspires, develops, and empowers them for a common goal.

Servant-leaders are not about ambition, titles, positions, or seeking to lead or to be seen; nor is it about seeking to be first among others. It is to give direction and to focus not on himself, but also on the people around him.

It takes one who has crucified his ego and pride to adopt this leadership style. (Galatians 2:20) The servant-leader, as a pioneer, goes ahead of others. He knows the destination and how to get there. He has the ability and the capability to move his people from where they are to where they should be. He is ready to make the necessary sacrifices to transform things from what is, to what should be.

The world and the Church need servant-leaders who will not only teach us how to fulfill our kingdom destinies but will by their examples, model excellence for us.

Characteristics of the Servant-Leader

The servant-leader submits his leadership to the Holy Spirit. His leadership is guided and controlled by the Holy Spirit and the Word of God. It's aimed at completing heaven's agenda, not man's. He is loyal and accountable to the Commander-in-Chief of heaven's army, Jesus Christ.

Considers It A Privilege to Serve

True servant-leaders consider leadership as an opportunity to bless to others and provide solutions to their problems. To them, leadership is a responsibility, not an opportunity to fulfill their vaulting ambitions or display their titles or achievements. It is their privilege to be like Jesus, who was not just the initiator of servant-leadership; He was the greatest servant-leader of all time.

Considers Others before Himself.

A servant-leader puts the interest of others before his. (Philippians 2:3) He cares more about the feelings of others than how they treat him. His first allegiance, as God's servant, is to the Lord.

Loves and Cares for the Flock

A servant-leader loves and cares for the flock. As is often said, "People don't care how much we know until they know how much we care." Servant-leaders have a shepherd's heart, more interested in feeding the flock, than in fleecing them. Their overall welfare is his major concern.

Humility

Humility is the hallmark of a true servant-leader. God has always been more interested in our heart attitudes than our performance that has no relevance to Him. Humility brings us to a point where we strip ourselves of our religious robes and titles and willingly serve others, not caring whether they are younger or older than us. A humble servant freely mixes with the rich and the poor, the high and the low. He does not think of himself more highly than he ought to think but counts others better than himself. (Philippians 2:3-4)

Does Not Lord It Over Others

If you are a servant-leader, you have no desire to lord over others. You neither abuse your authority nor campaign for positions, favor, fame or the respect of those you lead. You are not a dictator. You see those who work alongside you as partners or co-laborers in the Master's vineyard. You do not arrogate power and authority to yourself. Instead, you empower others and give them room and freedom to be themselves and to make useful contributions that will move the team forward.

Does Not Usurp Authority

Not inordinately ambitious, a true servant-leader is satisfied where God has placed him and will not usurp authority from those leaders God has placed him, no matter how inadequate their leadership might seem.

David found himself on two occasions in situations where Saul was at his mercy. (1 Samuel 24 and 26) He could have easily killed Saul to bring an end to threats to his own life. To have killed Saul would also have shortened the time he would have to wait before ascending the throne of Israel. But David chose not to kill Saul. He understood that God had anointed Saul and did not dare stretch out his hands against the king. That is the heart of a servant-leader.

Patiently Endures Trials and Temptations

In times of humiliation, persecution, hatred, rejection, and isolation, which invariably come, servant-leaders faithfully endure the hardship because of the dream God has given to them. They remain cool under pressure. They understand that such challenges are part of the process and their own preparation to get to the top.

Joseph was a good example of a servant-leader. He went from being a son to become a servant in Potiphar's house, and then to a prison before he was promoted to the throne. He faced assaults and false accusations. Though mistreated and humiliated, in the prison, his servant-heart could not be hidden.

Not selfish

A servant-leader is never selfish. Preferring to be "team-minded," he prefers the word "we" over the word "I." He understands that his main job is to ensure that the team functions effectively. He does not use his leadership position to run over anyone. Rather, he is sensitive to their needs and makes time to listen to them.

Has Integrity

A servant-leader is a person of integrity with unquestionable character. He is a man of his word, and so committed to the team that he becomes an inspiration to others. He is self-disciplined and consistent. It is impossible for him to instil discipline in other team members if he is not disciplined.

Waits on God for Promotion

It's not easy for any of us to wait for anything, especially a much-needed word from God. Because God generally moves slowly, we should remind ourselves that delay is not denial. We must keep trusting the Lord to visit us in due season, the set time for God's visitation. Through faith and patience, we will inherit the promise.

Always Willing to Serve

A servant-leader looks out for opportunities to serve. To him, to serve is more than an assignment, it's a way of life. He serves with zeal.

Does Not Seek Personal Gain

A servant-leader does not seek personal gain in serving the Lord. Like Paul, the apostle, He serves not out of necessity, but out of a deep love he has for the Lord and His work. He will not manipulate people or situations for selfish gain.

Does Not Seek the Commendation of Men

A servant-leader serves God and his people without concern for man's approval. Whether public ministry or private, he has no interest in the commendation of men. He walks before God and works with God with integrity of heart.

It Inspires Others

A servant-leader inspires his followers to attempt things they would never have thought possible for them to do. He is optimistic. He does not have to compel or coerce them.

Appreciates the Efforts of the Followers

A servant-leader recognizes the effort of those he leads. He values cooperation. From time to time, he praises, appreciates, and encourages them. He occasionally gives them unexpected tokens to express his appreciation to them for their jobs well done. Paul enjoins us in 1 Thessalonians 5:11 to *"Encourage one another and build each other up, just as in fact you are doing."*

A Good Follower

A major quality of servant-leaders is that though they are leaders, they are also excellent followers. (Matthew 8:9) They understand that to be a good leader, one must also be a good follower.

Has Excellent Work Ethic

God is a God of excellence. He does all things well and instructs us in Proverbs 22:29 to be skillful in our service. We are to be like him. Good work ethic goes with the spirit of excellence which involves wisdom, knowledge, counsel, power, diligence, devotion, discipline, competence, skill, stamina, supervision, and the fear of the Lord.

"Do you see a man skilled in his work? He will stand before kings; he will not stand before obscure men."

Saves People and Nations from Crisis

When there is a problem, a servant-leader will step in and try to solve it. He is concerned about the predicaments of other people.

Prepares Himself to Serve Well

No servant-leader can excel in his work without formal or informal training. While physical training is important to the success of your career, submit to the Holy Spirit's training as well. Allow Him to *make* you a servant-leader. Both Joseph and Nehemiah were prepared as servants in their closets before they were given opportunities to lead others.

Servant-leaders are good at producing other quality leaders like them. Their teams or groups rarely split because pride, the main cause of division, does not have a place in their lives. Their followers are loyal, and hardly ever rebel against them.

We are to take care of one another as we would want to be taken care of. If you are called to be a leader, this is the most excellent way to lead.

Chapter Four

NEEDED: TRAINED AND TESTED LEADERS

The world is looking for outstanding leaders with no skeletons in their closets to lead us out of the woods and out of darkness. We have many big name and big titled people, yet there remains an outcry for true leaders. God requires leaders.

God told Israel, concerning David, *"I have given him as a witness to the people, a leader, and commander for the people"* (Isaiah 55:4). God has raised you up as well. In every generation, there are more workers than leaders, because although an education will get you a job, it requires a commitment to continuous learning, investments of time, energy and resources that make you a leader. make a leader. The greatest display of leadership is service.

Concerning leadership, we have many characters in the Bible from whom we can learn. They include men like Joseph, Daniel, Moses, Nehemiah, and David. We see the development of leadership in each of their lives. For a more focused study, let's concentrate on the leadership abilities of Joseph, a child who through thick and thin finally assumed leadership in a foreign nation.

Joseph, who later became Prime Minister of Egypt, manifested some leadership traits from childhood. He supervised and observed what his elder brothers did, even though he was next to the youngest in the family. He wasn't one to overlook his elder brother's mistakes either. He brought reports back home.

His father saw that he was not an ordinary child and perceived leadership qualities in him. As a result, he made Joseph a coat of many colors. Although his brothers did not acknowledge it, the coat was a sign of royalty. With it, his father had prematurely prophetically made him a king in the house. But the problem with this "leader" was that he was still a teenager.

There are teenagers who are relatively mature and who behave as adults socially. Joseph didn't. He was quite immature in the way he interacted with his brothers. There was a prideful childish streak in him. It can be seen in the way he brought back evil reports to his father concerning his brothers. Today we would call him a "tattle-tale."

God knew, of course, that he was not ready to be the leader that he would one day be. He knew that his father had prematurely put him in a supervisory role and adorned him with a royal coat of many colors.

Joseph manifested some characteristics which are not concomitant with good leadership. He was a dreamer. The ability to work out a dream in life is one of the key elements of outstanding leadership. A leader who is not a dreamer is not a true leader. One cannot be a leader without dreaming, but it is one thing to dream in the spirit while sleeping; yet another thing to catch a vision of what God wants you to do and do it. One can be a manager or an administrator, but you cannot be a leader if you cannot dream. Although young Joseph, had all the leadership traits inherent in him, he was only a potential leader. He was a potential leader.

True leadership is a result of training and painstaking preparation. If you do not prepare to be a good leader, you will have settled for mediocrity, and should not expect excellent performance. You will have no standard and cannot evaluate whether you are making progress.

If your team is untrained, you likely have more problems than solutions. It's chaotic at times because as is said: "The man who does not know how to do his work quarrels with his tools." There is often a lot of quarreling among a team like that because there is no organized training that explains what each person is supposed to do, and how best to do it. Productivity or effectiveness comes from training.

When those who know and do their jobs well, you get the best. There will be no continuity where there is no standard training. One cannot transfer to others what he has not received. If many people around you are not well trained, or if perhaps a few people who understood the vision are no longer there, you are left with a generation that lacks understanding of the vision.

Benefits of Purposeful Training

Training has its own advantages. When you train people, you qualify them to function competently.

The more you train, the more confident they are in what they are doing. When you know who you are and what you are doing, you are no longer threatened or agitated by someone else's success. That is the only reason why you delegate tasks. You aren't concerned with who receives the credit.

But if you are untrained, you will want to do everything by yourself, and as a result, you will achieve very little.

Another good thing about training is that those who are trained to carry out their tasks can train others. The impact of proper training transcends generations. In 2 Timothy 2:2, Paul said to Timothy, *"and the things that thou hast heard of me among many witnesses, the same commit thou to faithful men, who shall be able to teach others also."* He wanted him to look for faithful men who would be able to teach others.

If you function among illiterates or people who are less educated than yourself, they may tend to feel threatened by your success. They may battle with feelings of inferiority which can affect their performance.

Joseph's Experiences were Part of His Training

God, knowing Joseph's destiny, did not choose to leave him to be raised by his father, lest he would have become a spoiled child. He allowed Joseph's brothers to plan for his death but did not allow them to kill him. When they placed Joseph in a pit, God made Judah uncomfortable with the situation, and he objected to their plan. "No! We can't kill our brother, let us sell him instead," Judah exclaimed. His suggestion looked good to them, and they sold Joseph. It was in the pit that Joseph was admitted into *The University of Suffering*, and there where he was given his first orientation. In the pit, you cannot look sideways or downward because there is nothing to see there. You are compelled to look upwards.

The training process is rarely pleasant. God brings you to the place where you can only look up and receive help. There in the pit, He began teaching Joseph to focus his attention on Him alone. In Psalms 121:1–2, David said, *"I will lift up mine eyes unto the hills, from whence comes my help. My help comes from the LORD, which made heaven and earth."* Afterwards, Joseph was sold as a slave, and taken from the pit to "The University of Egypt."

Joseph In *The University Of Egypt*

The vice-chancellor of the university was Potiphar, and his wife was head of department. Joseph had complete leadership training in that informal school. He had to learn servanthood before he could demonstrate leadership. His father's premature intervention in his life was rather to make him a ruler instead of a leader. God wants leaders, not rulers. His father was making him supervisor over his senior brothers, which made it obligatory for him to bring reports about his brothers' fieldwork. He did not have the heart of a leader, but that of a boss.

God wanted him to be a leader. He sent him to school where he became a servant. His masters made sure that he served them well.

They made him scrub the floor and tend the sheep. They sent him to the market to sell and bring back the money. He washed their linens and dressed their beds. These were chores his father would not have allowed him to do because he had servants and maids who did them in the house. God had to send him to a school where he could learn those things.

His head of department, Potiphar's wife, set an examination for him, which he passed. It was the exam of falling into the trap of adultery with her. She threatened his life when he refused to yield to her seductive advances. God helped him pass his examination. Then he went on to get his Master's Degree in prison. Thank God, he did not fail. He could have stopped at being a slave manager in the house of Potiphar, with which many people would be happy. But he passed his first-degree examination and proceeded for his Master's Degree.

Solve the Problems That Easily Get Your Attention

There are needs around you that you can identify which others may not notice. This suggests that you are expected to do something about them. Sometimes our dreams get actualized as we reach out to help others fulfill their dreams. Unless you interpret another person's dreams, your own dream may never come true. If you work hard just to fulfill your own dream, you may be hindering yourself from eventually seeing your dream come true. The way to make your dream work is to interpret the dreams of other people. Help others to become all they can be, and you will become all you can be. A true leader facilitates the raising of many. As a catalyst, he lifts others rather than put them down.

God wants you to be a showcase in which He can exhibit who He is to others. He wants to bless you in such a way that you will become a blessing. (Genesis 12:2-3) If you wish to prosper and make a meaningful impact, invest yourself in others. Flow, like a life-giving stream. Don't become a stagnant pond. The more you do, the more you will multiply your own blessings. The more you spread your resources abroad, the more it multiplies. Proverbs 11:24-25 confirms this:

> *"There is one who scatters, yet increases more, and there is one who withholds more than is right, but it leads to poverty. The generous soul will be rich, and he who waters will also be watered himself."*

To add value to others is to gain value in life. To make a difference in the lives of people is to rise in influence. Learn to serve others. Service can take you where status can't. Your value is determined by how many lives you have blessed. If you want to be a star that will shine brightly and be celebrated in your generation, be a servant. Look for opportunities to put smiles on the faces of others. *Everything God gives you is on its way to someone else when it reaches you. Your job is to make sure they get it.*

Jesus went about doing good and making a difference in the lives of people. He invested in relationships, touched lives, and left people better than He found them. He added value to their lives. The more you pour into the lives of others, the more influence you will command. David collected the worst human beings, worthless men and turned them into the mighty men of David. (1 Samuel 22:2) He invested in them, and they became useful to him in the day of battle.

To meet the needs of others is to have your own needs met. The Shunammite woman decided to meet a need in the life of the prophet and ended up meeting her own need of a child. She sowed into the anointing on Elisha's life and provoked the same anointing to fight her battle. *Your seed today handles your need tomorrow.*

When Joseph was in prison, he learned to serve not just his immediate master, but to serve his fellow prisoners. He interpreted their dreams. He likely prayed for and ministered to them in other ways.

He was there to serve. He did not see his state as demeaning but an opportunity to serve others. He said to one of his fellow prisoners, *"when you are restored to the kingdom, please remember me."* He came down so low that he was asking help from fellow prisoners. This is a mark of true humility. This was the man who was given a coat of many colors by his father. The first thing that God removed from him was his colorful coat. Immediately his brothers sighted him, they said, "See this dreamer." They went first for the premature coat his father gave to him. God was implying that it was too early to put the royal robe on him.

Meanwhile, Joseph did not understand what was going on. God was training him, so he would become the leader he was meant to be, to enable him to achieve his dreams. Had he stayed in his father's house, he would never have actualized his dream. His father could have pampered him and just kept him low. The process of becoming a leader is the process of humble service. That often means the Father's reducing us to something He can use.

God promised that he would humble the proud and exalt the humble. Each of us must go through the process of becoming a leader before we are exalted. There are no legitimate shortcuts. You must deliberately choose humility because you have the oil of leadership upon your life. God may choose to take you through a school of leadership. You may not like it. That was what happened to Joseph. By the time he completed his Master's program in the prison, he was ready to be deployed to the place where his dreams would finally be actualized.

There Is a Time to Train and A Time to Show Forth

When Joseph's training period was complete, God made a way for him to come before Pharaoh. God gave Pharaoh a dream, which no one at the palace could interpret. The king was told about Joseph's ability to interpret dreams of different kinds. He was brought before the

Pharaoh in his prisoner's attire. But when he rightly interpreted the Pharaoh's dream, they put a royal robe on him.

At last, he was qualified to wear the coat that his brothers had removed from him. The new coat and lots of other privileges were given to him through a chain of authority. Finally, his earliest dreams were coming true. His brothers, mother, and father eventually came to Egypt and bowed down to him. Everything he had seen in his early dream came to pass, but only because he had endured the training.

Often when going through these processes, if our faith in God is not strong, we begin to question God's intentions and integrity. We may even doubt His love for us. Some who submit to complaining will end up bitter. You can imagine a spoiled child now being the one doing everything that slaves do in the house, but Joseph went through the process with joy.

I am sure he also had a strong covenant relationship with God because when his master's wife tempted him, he said he could not do such a terrible thing in the sight of God. The issue here is about God. He held on to God despite all he went through. He refused to compromise his faith. He continually stayed the course, passed his examinations and stepped into his divinely ordained leadership role.

He was promoted to a very enviable position as the Prime Minister of Egypt. Except for the king, every other person submitted to him, including Potiphar, who had been the Vice-chancellor of his school during training. When Potiphar came before Joseph, he and his wife bowed down to him.

For God to trust you, He must train you. The Bible says that Jesus learned obedience by the things He suffered. Why would His Father make him suffer those things? He suffered so He could learn. There is a divine leadership school. Jesus went through that school and learned obedience. Moses also went through the school. David graduated from one of the toughest schools that any leader attend. No one is exempted from it.

Be A Unique Leader, Get Trained

Do not fuss over the appointment of someone's to a leadership role instead of you. If you are continually skipped over when leaders for various tasks are selected, it suggests that you have some more homework to do. Scripture declares that man's gift makes a way for him. Our gifts are developed and sharpened by training and experience. Could you imagine how a slave boy bought by a prison officer became the prime minister of a nation? His gift made a way for him. A process of purging was required to get him there.

Paul made it clear to Timothy that to be a leader is not enough. God looks for leaders with distinction. He told him that he could fit into one of these classes of leaders: a bronze leader, a silver leader or gold leader, depending on the amount of purging he was willing to go through. He encouraged him to desist from things that could reduce him to a mere vessel of clay or wood. Second Timothy 2:20–21 confirms this:

> *"In a great house there are not only vessels of gold and of silver, but also of wood and of earth; and some to honor, and some to dishonor; and that if a man, therefore,* purges himself from these, *he shall be a vessel unto honor, sanctified, and meet for the master's use, and prepared unto every good work."*

Training enhances our ability to skillfully multitask. It develops our mental capacity, even to process dreams, visions, and ideas. There were twelve apostles of Jesus Christ who preceded Saul of Tarsus, who became the apostle Paul. But apart from Luke, Paul seemed to be the most educated of them all, which helped him function better than others.

He wrote most of the books of the New Testament. He came in last but gave more to the church than those who preceded him. Do not quarrel with the process of leadership training. It may not be formal classroom training. It could be informal meetings with other leaders to give you an opportunity to meet and share ideas. Don't miss it.

Maximize Every Opportunity to Learn

We should continue to train and be trained. The moment we stop reading, learning, or training, we begin drifting backward in life. So, maximize every opportunity you must learn new things or add to your previous knowledge.

Every credible meeting offers something that will impact the attendees, be it a spiritual, academic, or social meeting. Never be in a hurry to seek a leadership position. If you are called to occupy one, and you are disposed to do so, go ahead; but do not fight for it. Train and prepare to lead, and the right positions will find you.

In preparation, you may be elected to a leadership role for which you are not yet qualified. This was the case with David. God sent Samuel to anoint him as the King of Israel. David's father did not nominate him at all. He never realized that his son David was qualified for such anointing, but God knew the training he had taken him through on the back side of the desert, and it made a way for him.

The world is dynamic, and change is constant. It will not wait for you. Stay abreast of new developments around you. Have you noticed that the communication pattern your children is different from yours? They have their own vocabulary and way of thinking.

The world is centered on change. Only the dead should not expect change. In the western world, many people write yearly professional examinations to remain relevant and be able to renew their professional licenses. In the Church, we rarely do so. Remember that once you stop training and learning, spiritual stagnation sets in. Once you become stagnant, your best efforts will be unproductive.

Chapter Five

QUALITIES OF A COMPETENT LEADER

A person should exhibit at least some leadership competency to qualify as a leader. In this chapter, we will look at some of the qualities of competent leaders.

He Has Foresight

A leader understands what lies ahead for him and his team. He can predict the path of progress and prepare his people in advance. He knows where everyone should go and understands the gap between where they are and where they should be. His unique abilities inspire the people sufficiently and motivate them to move from where they are to where they are supposed to be. This helps them follow his lead without complaining.

Every leader needs discernment to lead well. Discernment is the ability to see matters beyond the physical, using the enabling supernatural power of the Holy Spirit, or in some cases intuition. Discernment distinguishes the true from the false. It registers the content of one's heart, not the words they speak. A leader must be able to discern, otherwise, he and his followers lose. Discernment helps you avoid some problem prone transactions and puts you in a better position to settle issues between people. It also helps when you counsel with others.

He Is Vision Oriented

A leader must have a vision. Proverb 29:18 tells us that *"where there is no vision, the people perish."* A leader must have a picture of what he seeks to achieve in his mind. He must have a dream to pursue. He sees the destination with his mind's eye and leads his followers down the right paths to that destination.

Being able to define your vision is also very important. Your God-assignment is a trust from Him to make a difference in your world. You must clearly know and understand it to take people with you to the destination. Until your field is discovered and defined, your leadership potential can never have full expression. Discover your field and stay on it. Discover your place in God's master plan. (Jeremiah 29:11)

To know where you should be is a leader's responsibility. The people who are to be led should not have to worry about where they are going. The onus is on the leader to know and inspire them to leave where they are for where they should be without feeling they are paying too high a price. There are prices to be paid to attain new heights, but when correct leadership is in place, the people follow enthusiastically, willing to sacrifice if necessary.

The leader sets the goals and considers what to do to make his followers happy and willing to follow his lead. He needs to have the charisma, wisdom, and a love for people if he is to carry them along, without them falling by the wayside until the team achieves its goals. That is what leadership is about.

He Has Integrity

Integrity is a state of moral soundness or being unimpaired. It is adherence to a code of moral values, incorruptibility, being complete and undivided. As a leader, it is your responsibility to be honest and transparent with those you lead, aware your weaknesses and being able to compensate for them through training and experience. It is also the ability to use your strengths to inspire your people to be better than you.

Integrity involves honesty, transparency, openness, and freedom from hypocrisy. It starts in the heart but must become evident as you relate with people. It's the ability to keep one's word, one's sincerity in business, handling finances, keeping commitments, and loyalty. Psalm 15:1-4 and Hebrew 4:13 confirm this.

Leaders must also be honest and transparent in their relationship with God. As a leader, let your moderation be seen by all men. People should be able to take you at your word. Stand for righteousness and holiness. As you relate closely with the Lord, He will help you make the right decisions.

You cannot compromise your faith and teach your followers not to compromise theirs. You are a mirror to them. They believe and trust you, so they will confidently copy whatever they see you do. You need God's help to do it right, so you will not produce disciples that you will carry to hell because of compromise.

Leaders with integrity wear no masks. They do not fear scrutiny or exposure. They speak honestly and openly of themselves, which endears them to their followers and makes it easier for them to be trusted.

A good leader is just and handles people in the fear of God. There should be no room for favoritism. Some leaders make laws and fail to execute them when it has to do with their friends or relations. They are partial in executing justice. Emotions and sentimentality cloud their judgment.

Be fearless. Seek justice as if it were precious stones and execute it fearlessly. If you are fearless, you will be able to mete out justice to everyone without concern for who they are. Be bold and do not compromise your stand for righteousness. To please God and stand for righteousness should be uppermost in your heart. To be just, logically weigh the facts, and patiently rely on the Holy Spirit to help you make right decisions.

A servant-leader will be consistent in his standards and impartial in his dealings with people. No matter whose ox is gored, he will look at the issues objectively and critically before he draws conclusions or passes judgment. Never allow your emotions to take over when handling a serious issue. The way you relate to people goes a long way to attest to your fairness as a leader.

He Is Focused and Persistent

A quality leader is focused, and not easily distracted. He has a clear perception, understanding or direction concerning his vision. He can concentrate without distraction. If he decides to accept an assignment, no matter how hard it seems, he can succeed if he focuses his heart on it.

God knew that since man had His DNA in him, he has the willpower to accomplish anything he decides to do if only he remains focused. He overheard those who were building the Tower of Babel in Genesis 11:4-5, saw the focused determination in their hearts to build a tower to reach heaven, and said in verse six:

> *"...behold, the people is one, and they have all one language; and this they begin to do: and now nothing will be restrained from them, which they have imagined to do."*

Concentrate on whatever vision or assignment is entrusted to you; then do it so well that you are well known for it. There is no point being a "jack of all trades and master of none." God has equipped each of us to master our assignments. The light in our hearts will illuminate the world if we focus.

Focus will enable you to accomplish your vision. It will reduce distractions and enable you to lead others to accomplish a vision. The Apostle Paul was focused. In Philippians 3:14 he said: *"I press toward the mark for the prize of the high calling of God in Christ Jesus."*

Each of us has a kingdom potential, a purpose for which Jesus created and laid hold of us. To understand that purpose, and to focus on accomplishing it enables us to reach our kingdom potential. The world is full of opportunities waiting to be seized and maximized. Be your best self. There is no one else like you, and there never will be. Your potential and dreams are uniquely yours. Develop them to fulfill your destiny.

People are easily distracted from their pursuits in life. Learn to focus on the goal you are pursuing and resist distractions. Concentrate and become so adept in your field that anyone who needs your product or service will look for you. Check through the projects that sap your energy and resources. Find out what your major call in life is and channel your energy there. This will increase your success and relevance. Be decisive. Encourage, inspire, improve and multiply the good gifts you see in others. The field is crowded, but there is always room at the top for those willing to get there.

Famed Christian motivational speaker, the late Zig Ziglar often said, "I'll see you at the top." Head on up to the top, that's where you belong!

Persistence plays a major role to get you to the top. To persist is to move on resolutely or stubbornly despite oppositions. It is to insist on accomplishing a task or an enterprise, regardless of discouragement and counter influences. Persistence is the staying power, that keeps you on track through thick and thin, till you get to your destination. The same way stamps remain stuck on letters until they reach their destination, hang on to your vision until you see it actualized. Do not give up, your destination is closer than you think. Always dream big dreams, so that you will depend on God to help you accomplish them.

John Haggai once said, "Attempt something so great that it is doomed for failure unless God be in it." Nothing is impossible to a heart that is willing to dare. Persistence with purpose gives birth to progress and success. No matter the thorns that pierce your feet, see yourself already at your desired destination. If you can see it in your mind, you can reach it. Be determined to push aside every hindrance to achieve your goals.

Harold Sherman wrote a book titled *How to Turn Failures into Success*. In it, he gives the code of persistence as follows:

> "I will never give up as long as I know I am right, I will believe that all things will work out for me if I hang on to the end. I will be courageous and undismayed in the face of odds. I will not permit anyone to intimidate me or deter me from my goal."

He is Prayerful

Make room in your heart and your schedule for time alone with God. You cannot succeed as a leader without continual prayer. 1 Thessalonians 5:17 encourages us to *pray without ceasing*. Prayer is the breath of the believer. As important as air is for you to breathe physically, so prayer is for you to breathe spiritually. Leaders are often faced hard tasks and difficult decisions. You must not carry out those assignments in the flesh.

Make use of every opportunity to talk to God concerning yourself and the tasks entrusted to you. Without Him, you can do nothing. (John 5:19) Before you involve yourself with your daily activities, consult your Maker in prayer and release your daily duties to him. Involve Him in your decision making and in the execution of your assignments.

A leader must be prayerful. A praying leader will more likely be a competent leader. If Jesus was required to pray to remain a good leader, none of us can be a good a leader without a lifestyle of prayer. A prayerful leader will guide the people through life's rough waters if he does not want to sink the ship.

A prayerless leader is a powerless Christian, but a prayerful leader is a powerful leader. A powerless leader is in the devil's pocket to be used however he desires. But an effective prayer warrior is a powerful tool in God's hands to terrorize the devil and his cohorts. As the power of God comes upon you through prayer, you become a terror to the kingdom of darkness. God's power is not for fun. Through prayer, your voice will begin to ring with authority in both heaven and hell.

Signs and wonders follow a prayerful man's ministry. Tangible results are seen. He will live a stable Christian life, not tossed to and fro by every wind of doctrine, steadfast, unmovable, always abounding in the work of the Lord. Prayer attracts God's involvement. When He gets involved, He brings in His glory, affects everything.

Prayer releases God's power in people's lives and circumstances. It authenticates their preaching with signs and wonders. What's more, their words go forth with power to transform lives and convict men of sin, righteousness, and judgment. The words that proceed from their lips become "creative words" that produce results.

Constantly and consciously invite God into everything you do. Keep the communication line open between you and your Father in heaven. That way, you can get clear direction on issues before you make decisions. This will reduce the mistakes you make as a leader.

Issues that seem difficult or impossible, through prayer, are handled in the spirit realm and answered in the physical realm. While it is necessary for you to devote time to communing with God in your prayer closet, still make use of every available opportunity and place to stay connected to Him throughout your day. Sometimes, a little chat with Jesus can sort out challenging issues for you.

He Has Word Content

The extent to which you load your spirit man with God's Word will determine the measure or depth of heaven's revelation and glory you will carry. Your spiritual content affects both your visions and your actions. Divine revelation is first caught in the spirit before it's actualized in the physical. You need the Word of God to release God's revelation in your life. *"The entrance of His words gives light; it gives understanding to the simple"* (Psalm 119:130).

Allow the Word to flow into your spirit man. It will release spiritual light in you, so you can rise and shine. Your depth of revelation in God's Word will determine how far you will go in your walk with God. Knowledge of God's Word will enrich your prayer life. (Colossians 3:16) What the devil and life's challenges bow to God's Word, not ours. It should dwell richly in our hearts. We are to meditate on God's Word and declare it day and night. His Word is life! John 6:63 reiterates this saying:

> *"It is the spirit who gives life, the flesh profits nothing, the words that I have spoken to you, they are spirit, and they are life."*

Ensure that you hear His voice daily by reading His Word. Set aside time in your busy schedule to study God's Word. Hide it in your heart to keep you from sinning. (Psalm 119:11, 105; Joshua 1:8) If you do not value His Word, you do not value Him. If you are not personally connected to Him through his Word, you have no future with Him. If you listen for His voice daily, you and your destiny are secure.

He Is People Oriented

You cannot be a leader without touching people's lives. Before you become a leader, your success is about you. But once you become a leader, your success is about how you can help others succeed. To lead others to succeed, you must first become their friend. Be friendly and you will attract people. Invest in their success and help them to become the best they can be. Many lives may be touched from a distance, but some must be touched at close range. Be patient with people. Study them to know how to carry everyone along and ensure that they maximize their potential. Genuinely love them.

Look for ways to add value to people's lives, bless them, make them smile, bring them joy, and ease their burdens. Show concern for their well-being, not just for what they can offer you. You are of greater value if you give people more than you take from them. Typically, what you receive from people will be determined by what you've sown into their lives. To the extent you go to serve them and sacrifice on their behalf is often the extent to which they will be willing to lay down their lives for you.

Your worth as a leader is not determined as much by the number of people who serve you, but by the number of people you serve. When people are assured of your love for them, they will not only listen to what you have to say but will gladly do what you ask of them. When you get their hearts, you can get their pockets, their assets, and the potential they hold.

To relate well with others is the best asset you can possess. We sharpen each other as iron sharpens iron. The extent to which you attract people in your life is the extent to which you can improve yourself. But don't only aim at enriching yourself. Build others. The more successful your relationships, the more fulfilled you will be. The more practical results will be seen in your life. Even your finances will improve. As you add value to others, more value will be added to you. There is nothing more fulfilling than to be instrumental in somebody else's success story.

Allow plenty of room in your heart for all kinds of people. Don't try to force everyone who hangs out with you to fit into your mold. Encourage them to be themselves and become the best versions of themselves. As God does, love them like they are.

He Is Humble

An Apostolic leader humbly accepts himself as God sees him. He recognizes his abilities, inabilities, and unworthiness in the light of God's greatness and mercy, regardless of his achievements. Humility is the pathway to promotion. (Proverbs 15:33) Humility attracts God's blessings and grace. We are reminded in James 4:6 that God resists the proud but gives grace to the humble. A humble heart is the secret of greatness with God and with man. God hates pride. He has promised that He will exalt the humble and resist the proud.

- Humility recognizes God's grace in the lives of others and credits them with their accomplishments and contributions. A humble leader will acknowledge God in his affairs and consciously give God glory for whatever He gives him or accomplishes through him. He makes pleasing God, his priority.

- A humble leader will go the extra mile, and joyfully do things others will refuse to do. Often one can't simply instruct people as to what to do, he must also show them how to do it.

- Jesus, our model of humility, taught His disciples in Matthew 11:29 saying, "*Take my yoke upon you, and learn of me; for I am meek and lowly in heart: and ye shall find rest unto your souls.*"

In Mark 10:42, Jesus said, *"The rulers of this world lord it over their citizens and subjects, but it is not so in the kingdom of God. He who wants to be the greatest must be a servant of all."*

- Humility isn't stupidity or timidity. It is not about degrading or oneself before others. Rather, it's the awareness and acceptance of one's true value. It's not about allowing yourself to be trampled on, or denied your rights. It's simply being self-confident and esteeming others better than yourself.

  Humility credits God with one's successes rather than taking credit oneself. If blessed with prosperity and fame, a good leader will use those things freely to bless others.

He is Knowledgeable

A good leader knows through study and experience, more than most of those who he leads. The quality of one's life is determined by the level of their knowledge and references. Good leaders are readers. By reading, he takes advantage of the knowledge and experiences of others. When one stops learning, he will stop growing and soon become irrelevant. Keep your mind sharp by continually reading good material. Commit to learning and you'll elevate your leadership.

Information is important to every leader. It is the fuel of every vision. To know where one is going is important. To know how to get there is even more important. The measure of your value for knowledge determines the quality of your leadership. Knowledge alone will not make you a leader, but without it, you cannot become one.

As a leader, you should build a quality personal library. Great leaders will gladly sacrifice to gain knowledge. Leaders read their way to greatness. Forget wisdom without knowledge, because wisdom is the application of knowledge. Knowledge is what you have discovered to be right.

Knowledge begins with knowing God. Daniel 1:12 states that it is our knowledge of God that enables us to do exploits for Him. Many know the acts of God and see them. But they do not truly know God's ways.

It was knowing God's ways that distinguished Moses from the Children of Israel. Psalms 103:7 records that *"He made known his ways to Moses, his deeds to the people of Israel.* Moses knew God's ways because He spent time with God and because in Exodus 33:13 he asked God to reveal His ways to him. The Children of Israel knew what God did. Moses knew why God did it.

The depth of your knowledge of God will determine how you process through each season of your life. To know the times and seasons of one's life in God's calendar will help him settle issues in the spirit and at times, to calm life's raging storms. A man who understands life's seasons will never be ruled by his circumstances but will follow God's leading day by day.

The level of your knowledge of your field helps you become known as an expert. If you do not try to learn more in your field, you will limit yourself from reaching your ultimate potential. Acquire all the professional information you can to become the best in your field.

Have an insatiable hunger for knowledge. Ignorance will hinder you. Proverbs 1:22b tells us that fools hate knowledge. It's true that ignorance will prevent you from reaching your kingdom destiny. If you are ignorant of who you are, and all God has invested in you to make a difference in your world, your destiny will be truncated and possibly aborted. Hosea 4:6 states it this way. *"My people perish for lack of knowledge."* Proverbs 25:2 tells us that *"it is the glory of God to conceal a matter, but it is the honor of Kings to search out a matter."*

We have been ordained as kings and priests unto our God. (Revelation 1:6) It is an honor to us when we search out and discover God's hidden wisdom. *"The secret things belong to the Lord; the things that are revealed belong to us"* (Deuteronomy 29:29). *"The secret things of the Lord are for those who fear him"* (Psalms 25:14). The kingdom of God is filled with mysteries which God in His mercy chooses to reveal to those who are dear to Him. Jesus told his disciples in Luke 8:10, "*Unto you, I give the keys of the Kingdom, but to those who are outside, everything is in parables.*"

Mysteries are hidden with God and can only be revealed to us through the Holy Spirit, who searches the mind of God according to 1 Corinthians 2:10-13:

> *"But God has revealed it to us by his Spirit. The Spirit searches all things, even the deep things of God... In the same way, no one knows the thoughts of God except the Spirit of God."*

Strive to learn more each day. Have a continual quest for knowledge. Keep reading and asking questions. Great men of destiny sharpen their minds through books. The books you read will determine who you become. As you read good books, written by great men who have gone before you, you will discover the secrets of their success, their wisdom, and thinking patterns. This will help develop your brain and enable you to see areas of your life that need growth, so you can become the best you can be.

The more you learn, the more relevant you will become to your world. No wonder 2 Timothy 2:15 encourages us to *"Study to show thyself approved unto God, a workman that does not need to be ashamed, rightly dividing the word of truth."* Keep learning, keep leading, keep fresh, and remain relevant.

A good leader will have a knowledge of God and His Word. It is one thing to know *about* God, another to *experience* Him. You must know God and His Word personally to know His will and His ways. An awareness of what you don't know and haven't learned from God is a great advantage. If a person is unconscious of what he does not know, he'll make no effort to learn. In turn, he won't grow or flow to bless others. His life will be as a stagnant pool, poisoning others, rather than a spring-fed fresh life-giving stream the quenches their thirst.

A leader must not be a novice. He must be someone who has experienced life. This will make him less likely to suffer casualties.

He Is Full of Wisdom.

Wisdom cannot be overemphasized. Proverbs 4:5-7 states:

"Get wisdom! Get understanding! Do not forget, nor turn away from the words of my mouth. Do not forsake her, and she will preserve you; Love her, and she will keep you. Wisdom is the principal thing; Therefore, get wisdom. And in all your getting, get understanding."

Wisdom will enable you to use the knowledge God has endowed you with to carry out your life vision and reach your goals. Everyone has challenges in life and occasionally suffers mishaps. Two of the differences between individuals are their ability to learn from their experiences, and how they use that knowledge to get them to their destiny. What you know won't make sense to everyone, but it will make your life better and more impactful.

Despite all you know, if you cannot use it to produce results in that will, in turn, make the world better, you are not wise. Results should be practical. Your wisdom should produce specific effects in the lives of the people around you. You should be able to watch them grow from strength-to-strength, level-to-level, and move from wherever they were when they met you to the place they aspire to be.

A leader should be wise. Wisdom will be required to handle leadership matters. Wisdom is a valuable treasure that will guarantee a great future. It is acquired by high-level self-discipline. He must not be a novice. Instead, a competent leader must be mentally mature. Not necessarily physical age. He should have experience in what he is doing. A know-it-all will never succeed.

Every good leader in the Bible felt inadequate, which is why they relied on God's ability. Wisdom will enable you to use your knowledge to bring practical solutions to challenges facing your team. It is one thing to know your duties yet another thing to know how to carry them out. God is the source of Godly wisdom. His foolishness is said to be wiser than the wisest of men. God's wisdom, which is a mystery, is the gateway to a glorious destiny.

All we need to direct our Christian lives and ministries is embedded in wisdom. The measure of your impact is determined by how much you affect your world. You must learn to focus your attention on things that produce results.

Wisdom, like a latent energy, comes alive when God's Spirit breathes on it. Jesus is the personification of God's wisdom. Wisdom is the acquisition and intelligible application of knowledge to your situation that gets results. (Job 28:12-18) Revelation gives you access to depth. Wisdom, applied knowledge, gives you access to the application of the revelations you have received.

Wisdom is the costliest virtue in the kingdom. It is the commodity of greatest value; a genuine treasure that guarantees a great future. One acquires wisdom through a high level of personal discipline. You cannot talk of wisdom without knowledge.

Daniel 12:3 says, *"the wise shall shine forever and ever."* Wisdom provides you access to the secrets of God that makes eternal stars. You have the potential to be sound, but you need the wisdom of God to be fired up into action. Wisdom helps you to excel above the natural. Wisdom gives you the capacity to generate radical solutions to plaguing problems and enables you to make sound decisions. Wisdom brings witty inventions, beyond natural imagination.

Wisdom is needed for continual breakthroughs. It mysteriously moves you to your promised land. It was the rocket that translated Joseph from the prison to the palace in Genesis 41:34-40. Daniel would not have been supernaturally sought for and prospered under three regimes without wisdom. Wisdom is the principal thing and understanding will make you outstanding in every area of life. Joshua excelled because he was filled with the spirit of wisdom. (Deuteronomy 34:9)

Wisdom achieves impossible results and identifies opportunity in adversity. (Job 28:7-28) Wisdom, a heavenly treasure, your most valuable asset, will turn the desert into a garden. It is an incomparable solution-bearing force that's available in God. No intellectual capability can produce wisdom. (Daniel 4:8-9; Daniel 5:11-12; and Daniel 6:3) It is far beyond mere intellectual exertion. Nothing will distinguish you like the spirit of wisdom. It will empower your mind for discretion and enable you to make right decisions. (Psalm 112:5; Proverb 8:12)

Wisdom is inventive. It can generate practical solutions. (Deuteronomy 34:9) Wisdom puts you on the way of pleasantness and the paths of peace. Wisdom will grant you access into the secret depths of God's Word and provide you with the proper application of the revelations you receive.

Benefits of Wisdom

- **Wisdom is a defense.**

    "For wisdom is a defense as money is a defense, But the excellence of knowledge is that wisdom gives life to those who have it" (Ecclesiastes 7:12).

- **Wisdom puts a glow on your face that stands you out among many.**

    "Who is like a wise man? And who knows the interpretation of a thing? A man's wisdom makes his face shine, And the sternness of his face is changed" (Ecclesiastes 8:1).

    Also, Daniel 12:3 says, *"Those who are wise shall shine like the brightness of the firmament."*

- **Wisdom releases wealth to as many as love her**

    "Riches and honor are with me, Enduring riches and righteousness. My fruit is better than gold, yes, than fine gold, and my revenue than choice silver. I traverse the way of righteousness, In the midst of the paths of justice, that I may cause those who love me to inherit wealth, that I may fill their treasuries" (Proverbs 8:18-21).

- **Wisdom prolongs life**

    "Length of days is in her right hand, in her left hand riches and honor.... She is a tree of life to those who take hold of her, and happy are all who retain her" (Proverbs 3:16, 18).

- **Wisdom gives direction.**

    "If the ax is dull, and one does not sharpen the edge, then he must use more strength; but wisdom brings success" (Ecclesiastes 10:10). Wisdom is a spiritual compass that will navigate you to your destiny.

He Is Courageous

Courageous people do not focus on their fears, but on the task at hand and how to accomplish it. Courage is the ability to confront and conquer your fears, while you effectively carry out your tasks. Do not allow fear to paralyze and prevent you from accomplishing your task.

Courage is the ability to forge ahead and fulfill your destiny in spite of your fears or other challenges. Do not allow your fears to determine the choices you make in life. Deal with your fear by facing your task with focus and determination to do it well. Instead of allowing your fears to stop you, allow it to pull out the great potential you possess. Courage enables you to take risks and attempt seemingly impossible challenges.

Instead of allowing such situations to throw you off balance and intimidate you, courageously confront and attempt to resolve them. Even when an action does not make sense to your human mind, and you know that God expects you to do it, courage says go, and it helps you step over all obstacles and emerge victorious on the other side.

It requires courage to be different and to stand alone. Yet a courageous man is in the majority because he will attempt what others, because of fear, won't. It takes courage to smile at the storm and be strong when going through hard times, knowing full well that His presence is with you. Isaiah 43:2 confirms this:

> *"When you pass through the waters, I will be with you;*
> *And through the rivers, they shall not overflow you.*
> *When you walk through the fire, you shall not be burned,*
> *nor shall the flame scorch you."*

Courage will make you a pacesetter, a trailblazer, a pathfinder and a pioneer. (Proverbs 21:20) It will make you a reformer and a transformer. Those who want to be like everyone else never emerge as the pacesetters. To make maximum impact on your generation and leave your footprints on the sand of time, you must seek to be different and stand out from others. When you lack the courage to do so, you succumb to the norms. Courage puts you on the path of greatness. The ability to persevere under tough conditions makes a leader stand out among his peers. A competent leader does not give up easily in the face of challenges.

Every leader must be a fighter. You must be courageous otherwise you won't accomplish anything. God is always in need of courageous men who will partner with Him to release upon the earth the new things in His heart.

Don't fear what others think or say about situations around them. Honor God in your heart and step out in faith to accomplish the extraordinary. Courage helps you to stand for God through thick and thin. It helps you to obey God and boldly carry out His instructions without being afraid of the consequences of your actions. That is why in commissioning Joshua, Moses said to him in Joshua 1:6-9:

> *"Be strong and of good courage, for to this people you shall divide as an inheritance the land which I swore to their fathers to give them. Only be strong and very courageous, that you may observe to do according to all the law which Moses My servant commanded you..."*

He Is Diligent

An apostolic leader must be physically and mentally strong to be able to multitask. He must be able to deliver under pressure. Nobody can be a high flyer in any field without being a hard worker. Input determines output in any field. The quality of your labor defines the limits of your future. Only those who care to go the extra mile produce extraordinary results. Your performance rating defines your leadership rating.

To walk the extra mile helps you rise to an extraordinary place in your field. You cannot be truly successful without hard work. Your perception of work will determine the level of stamina you will apply to it. See work as a challenge, and work completed as an accomplishment.

In His parable of the talents in Matthew 25:14-30, Jesus warned against laziness. In verses 26-32, He sharply rebuked the third servant who was so lazy and wicked that he did not use his talent. He chose to die with all the potential God had endowed him rather than to bless his generation.

He Is Committed to His Vision

A competent leader is one committed to whatever vision is entrusted into his hands. Commitment has to do with a stubborn, unstoppable, irrevocable resolve to pursue a cause or a goal to a successful end. (Daniel 3:1-11) It is a deep pressing desire to pursue your vision to its actualization.

Without commitment, you cannot become a quality leader. You must first be committed to a cause before you can persuade other people to join your pursuit of it. Commitment should be total and entire. When you are committed to a vision, the following things are evident:

1. Everything else loses its attraction to you.
2. You have courage to attempt the impossible. You see no task as impossible.

3. You will gladly sacrifice money, time, energy, comfort, property, engagements, and pride. Death loses its power over your life. (Daniel 4:17)
4. Impossible doors swing open before you. (Esther 4:16)
5. Onlookers behold your commitment and draw near to God.
6. Your fear bows to your commitment.
7. Immovable mountains are moved at your words.
8. Greater value is given to your pursuit because of your commitment.
9. Heaven and earth acknowledge you, the world gives you attention, heaven answers you speedily, and hell is terrorized at your presence.
10. Exhaustion and weariness cannot keep you from accomplishing your task.

He Is Filled with The Holy Spirit

A leader should be filled with the Spirit of God. Without being filled with the Holy Spirit, he will be deficient in many ways. He may hardly receive guidance from the Spirit of God. The Bible says, *"For as many as are led by the Spirit of God, they are the sons of God."* One of the criteria that was used in the selection of New Testament leaders was the infilling of the Holy Ghost.

Stephen met this criterion, and he was selected from among the people to direct a food disbursement committee. (Acts 6:1-6) A good leader also shows group loyalty. He must do for the people what he wants them to do for him. As a leader, be there for your people, and they will be there for you.

He Has Strong Faith in God

A good leader possesses a large measure of faith. There are different classes of faith: strong, little, weak and dead faith. He must have a strong faith in God. According to the Bible, whatever is not done by faith is sin.

In Hebrews 11:6, the Bible says, *"But without faith, it is impossible to please him: for he that cometh to God must believe that he is and that he is a rewarder of them that diligently seek him."*

Faith is the realization that God makes seemingly impossible things possible. Godly men and women of old were people of faith; and people of substance. Out of nothing, they knew God would do something. They started with nothing, but by faith, they accomplished much for God.

He Is A Good Communicator

Effective communication is the bedrock of team leadership. To make significant progress, a leader must communicate effectively with his followers. When communication breaks down, there is chaos. A good leader is a good negotiator, diplomatic, always speaking the truth.

People prefer to follow one who will listen to them, which is why to be a good leader one should be a good listener. He will provide an effective method to receive feedback from team members. As a leader listens to his people, he can understand their challenges and can find ways to help them. Sadly, in some cases, some hurting people choose to keep to themselves because their so-called leader does not have the time for them.

He Is Charismatic and Encouraging

A good leader should be enthusiastic, dynamic and full of life or the morale of his followers could be affected. He must be smart and act swiftly when and where necessary because at times delay may be dangerous. He cannot be given to procrastination.

A good leader can empathize with those who are hurting. He spurs his team members on, even in their most discouraging moments. He strives to bring out the best in people and encourages the faint-hearted while gently restraining the over-zealous. The leader must be positive in his contributions and plans. Being positive about the group's vision helps strengthen his company of followers. Optimism drives people forward in whatever they do.

A competent leader will reconcile clashing viewpoints rather than take sides. He inspires his people to follow. He delegates responsibilities but does not abdicate. He appreciates his follower's efforts when they do well and lovingly rebukes them when they are wrong. He accepts people's ideas and suggestions and goes out of his way to encourage them. He inspires confidence in them by believing in them and acknowledges each person's contribution to the common effort.

He recognizes the good qualities in those working with him and channels their strengths in areas of their giftedness. He makes his people feel needed and important. He encourages a team spirit that discourages cliques and realizes that people have different backgrounds, upbringings, exposures, and trainings. He doesn't expect everyone to be like himself.

He Is Disciplined

Discipline is your ability to train your mind and character to obey certain codes of conduct that will help you fulfill your destiny. As you submit to your training you will shape your mental faculties and develop moral character.

Discipline is also defined as self-imposed guidelines and restrictions to achieve a desired goal. The disciplinary culture of the followers in most cases reflects the leader's level of discipline. A disciplined leader inspires disciplined followers. He comes to meetings regularly and arrives on time--if not early. The leader who has the habit of strolling into meetings after the stipulated time is mostly viewed as disrespecting his people. They will most likely follow his poor example.

Dignity is a product of discipline. Excelling in your calling is a product of high-level self-discipline. Discipline helps you to carry out your tasks with utmost efficiency. In 1 Corinthians 9:23-27 Paul mentioned how he became all things to all men, so he could at least win some. He also consciously disciplined his body and brought it under subjection so that after preaching to others, he would not be a castaway.

He Is Courteous

Courtesy is the hallmark of every good leader. A leadership position is not given to us so we can lord it over our followers. You can be the leader of all, but you must still be the one who respects all. An old English slogan says, "When you respect another person, he reciprocates." Competent leaders lead by example, sows the right seed, and expects his followers to do the same.

Your inner person is very important. People can sense the depth of your character as they interact with you.

> "The only thing that walks from the tomb with the mourners and refuses to be buried is the character of a man. This is true. What a man is, survives him. It can never be buried." --J. R. Miller

Therefore, a leader's temperament must be Spirit-controlled. Your attitude and character should not prevent people from coming close to you, and you should not expect others to do what you are unwilling to do. A competent leader leads from the front. He is not afraid to be involved and to be at the forefront of what he believes. He initiates things.

He Is Mentally Objective

As a competent leader, you should be objective and not allow your biases and personal perceptions to affect your decisions. Even if the whole world is going in one direction, do not go with the majority. It is not often that they carry the vote. Be convinced before you make major decisions. Try to analyze situations carefully, make objective, independent decisions and communicate them respectfully.

A leader is expected to offer solutions to problems that would not cause resentment or discourage his followers. He may not have the answer to the need at the time, but he should be able to harness other team members' wealth of experience in handling the challenges he encounters.

A leader must handle criticism objectively. Every leader will be criticized, even those who are dead. If his team is not doing well, he should take responsibility for the team's failure. Some people are afraid to say, "I am sorry, I don't know how that happened." A leader should not be quick to cast blame on others but should take responsibility for mistakes made by his team members and do his best to correct them. A leader says, "We are sorry about what happened and will seek a way to remedy it."

He Is A Good Follower

Every competent leader should be a good learner and a follower. Remember, no one is born a leader; you grow into positions of leadership. However, before you attain that height, you need to learn submission and loyalty to those in authority over you. If you are not a good follower, you cannot be a good leader. A good leader must be able to teach others and impact their lives. Paul told Timothy to raise leaders who would be able to teach and raise other leaders. (1 Timothy 2:2)

He Has an Excellent Spirit.

He must have an excellent spirit like Daniel. Personally, I am more comfortable working with people who may not have much knowledge or experience, and have a beautiful spirit, than those who are versatile and experienced but have a bad spirit. Some people are good at many things, but their spirit is disturbing. The way they relate to people usually creates an atmosphere of chaos around them. They may work very well at times, but the trouble they cause outweighs the value of their work. You don't only need skill, but you should have a sweet spirit and be a blessing to others as well.

People celebrate your presence because of your excellent spirit, not necessarily because of what you know or what you can do for them. A leader must be innovative and dynamic. People feel bored when the leader does not have anything new and inspiring to offer.

Habitually Friendly and Full of Love

Friendliness is one virtue required in good leadership. Although it is impossible to be intimately close to everyone around you, you must be kind to all. A competent leader loves and cares for the flock and calls them by name. He gets to know them intimately and has personal relationships with them. When you are friendly to your team members, you easily motivate them. When you love the people you lead, you and they will accomplish great results.

Obviously, if you pastor or lead hundreds of people, your ultimate familiarity will be with a limited number of folks. Your role will be to relate intimately with them and be a model they can emulate. You, in that case, lead the leaders.

He is Joyful and Happy

A leader must be a happy person. Nobody wants an angry man or a "sad sack" around him, let alone to be his leader. People want to follow someone who exhibits the joy of the Lord.

The devil would rather steal your joy than your possessions. Without joy, you cannot enjoy life. Don't let him steal your joy. Christianity does not require you to abandon every enjoyable thing. Lighten up and don't be too intense about life. Stop trying to reason out and analyze everything in your life.

Trust God to take you to where you desire to be in His time. You may not have reached your promised land, but rejoice that you have left your Egypt, and are making significant progress in your journey. Enjoy each step of the journey. Don't wait until you reach the destination. Celebrate the spiritual and physical victories along the way. Determine to keep your peace, no matter what you are going through.

Have fun in your relationship with God and with people. You are responsible for your joy. Do not yield that responsibility to anyone else. Make up your mind to be happy and to enjoy life. The Holy Spirit is the oil of joy and gladness, He is the Spirit of joy and rejoicing and facilitates your access to revelation and the path of life. People who rejoice do not lack access to revelation.

Health and vitality are in found in joy. Proverbs 18:14 makes it clear that when your heart is broken, it dries your bones and breaks down your body. Joyful people go from strength to strength, constantly rejoicing before God. (Nehemiah 8:10) As you rejoice in the Lord, revelations, wealth and vitality, keep flowing. You enjoy divine presence, and it strengthens your heart. Joy, a treasure from heaven, is your most valuable asset. It is the spiritual sickle with which you reap your harvest from every seed sown.

Too many Christians are on their way to heaven but aren't enjoying the journey. They make it boring and intense. Lighten up and enjoy the ride. The heaven you are going to is not a boring place. It is full of life, fun and exciting activities. Learn to enjoy your life here on earth, so that it will not be strange for you to do so in heaven.

God desires to put smiles on our faces daily. *"In His presence is fullness of joy and at His right hand are pleasures forevermore"* (Psalm 16:11b).

Jesus said in John 10:10, *"The devil comes to kill, steal and destroy, but I came that you may have life and have it more abundantly."*

John 15:11 emphasizes it. Jesus said to his disciples, *"These things I have spoken to you, that my joy may remain in you, and that your joy may be full."*

A merry heart does good like medicine. (Proverbs 17:22) You are the architect of your joy. Don't give it to another. When your heart is merry, you release joy to others who come your way. Touching people's lives and making it more pleasant and enjoyable is of great price before the Lord. Anytime you have an opportunity to invest in someone's life, put a smile on their face, exhort or encourage them or make them feel better, that is a great thing before the Lord.

A lot of our health challenges are a result of stress. When you hang out with unhappy people, refuse to allow their sadness to affect your joy and mess up your day. God wants you happy in the world, enjoying the life He gave to you, refusing to be miserable and frustrated.

He Has A Positive Disposition

The mind is the battlefield in Spiritual warfare. That is where we win or lose our battles with the enemy of our soul. If you win in your mind, then you will win physically. The primary place the devil attacks you is in your mind. He attacks your relationship with people and the assignments in your hands through your mind. He wants you see something wrong with people with whom you relate so he can mess up your relationships with them.

Your mind is a major gateway into your spirit. Proverbs 4:23 encourages us to guard our hearts with all diligence, for out of it comes the issues of life. Your thoughts are the seeds that create your attitudes that become the actions that you take. What you think and meditate on becomes a reality in your life. The quality of your thoughts determines and affects the quality of your life and ministry. That which occupies your mind will determine who you become.

The life you are now living is the result of the thoughts you have meditated on in the past and the words you've spoken. Proverbs 23:7 confirms that *"as a man thinks in his heart, so is he."* Your thinking is reflected in your body language, actions, and words. It can make you sad or happy, can encourage, discourage or depress you. Your thoughts affect what you say, for out of the abundance of the heart, the mouth speaks (Luke 6:45). Although you are not necessarily responsible for your thoughts, you *are* responsible for your thinking. You must erect a solid immigration control at the door of your mind and not allow your thoughts to run wild.

God gave clear prescriptions in His word of the kind of thoughts you should entertain: thoughts that are *true, noble, right, pure, admirable, of good report, excellent and praiseworthy.* (Philippians 4:8). When thoughts that do not fit into God's list enter your mind, you must take them captive, and consciously replace them with thoughts that do line up with God's Word.

He Is Open to Correction and Counsel

We all know in part, and we see in part. It is only God that has the complete picture. We need each other because no one individual is an island. Whatever we are today is because of the input of many people. The best way to grow up is to be open to correction. From time to time, we all need rebuke and/or correction. A proud person hates to be corrected, but the humble person will earnestly receive and profit from it.

The best gift you can have is mature friends and well-wishers who will tell you the truth about yourself. Such friends are great treasures. Do not toy with them. They will help you become who God wants you to be and go where He wants you to go. One who is seldom criticized or corrected will lack the platform or impetus for growth. Proverbs 27:5-6 confirms this:

> *"Open rebuke is better than secret love, the rebuke of a friend is better than the kisses of an enemy. Harsh discipline is for him who forsakes the way, and he who hates correction will die."* (Proverbs 15:10)

He Opens His Mouth with Wisdom

Successful leaders do not speak before they think. They often process information in their minds, then choose their words because words are very powerful. They can encourage, discourage and destabilize. Words are not just sounds released into the air. They convey meanings, send messages and affect personalities. They can bless, or cause pain. They affect both the speaker and the hearer. They are shaping tools used to make personalities and situations what we want them to be. They kill or give life, are poisonous or medicinal. You become what you say, and those around you become what you tell them. The words you speak are very effective in the realm of the spirit and affect what happens in the physical.

Your words can affect your whole life, especially your health. They can produce a harvest of mood swings and changes in character. The following scriptures confirm the power behind the words you speak.

"Life and death lie in the power of the tongue..." (Proverbs 18:21).

"He who will love life and see good days, let him refrain his tongue from evil and his lips from speaking lies" (1 Peter 3:10).

"There's that speaks like the piercing of the sword, but the tongue of the wise promotes health" (Proverbs 12:18).

"The mouth of the righteous is a well of life. But violence covers the mouth of the wicked" (Proverbs 10:11).

"Open your mouth with wisdom, and let kindness rule your tongue" (Proverbs 31:26; Ephesians 4:29).

Use your words to build up, not to destroy, pull or tear down. They should not paralyze your spouse. Let them heal, restore, mend and repair any damage created. We respond better to compliments than to criticism.

Put life into your conversations with people; mingle it with jokes and humor, even when discussing very serious matters. In communication, note that your words form only 7%, your tone 38%, and your body language 55%. Those who are poor listeners and fast talkers are not good communicators. James 1:19 admonishes us to *"be quick to hear, slow to speak and slow to become angry."*

He Is Impartial

A leader must not show partiality. Deuteronomy 1:17 states this clearly: *"do not show partiality in judgment...."* Be fair with all people. Always hear both sides of a matter before drawing conclusions. Proverbs.18:13 and 17 also confirm this:

> *"He who answers a matter before listening, to him it is folly and shame. The first to present his case seems right until another comes forward and questions him."*

Effective leaders do not judge matters without first making thorough investigations. Proverbs 24:23 says: *These things also belong to the wise: It is not good to show partiality in judgment.* Justice is the foundation of God's throne.

He Is Able to Manage Himself and His Task

Leadership is the product of efficient "self-management." If you cannot manage yourself, you cannot manage others, or the tasks entrusted to you. Every good leader should be able to manage his potential to yield the highest dividend to his generation. This is the best way to give your leadership expression. There is a lot inside you waiting to be made manifest in your world.

According to Matthew 5:13-15, we are the salt of the earth, needed to give taste to the tasteless world and to bring healing to the decaying situations around us. We are to be assets to our world, not liabilities; light in the darkness, pacesetters, showing others the way to go. Leadership begins with you, and you must be able to manage yourself. That means you must know who you are, know where you are going and what it takes to get there, commit yourself to getting there and going the extra mile if necessary.

God is the author of leadership who will give you the platform to validate your leadership. It is your efficient management of this task that culminates in leadership. He told Adam to have dominion, blaze the trail, be in charge and direct the affairs of the earth. He showed him how to manage the garden to validate his leadership.

Search for relevant resource materials that will help you excel in your field. Draw up a program for your personal and spiritual development through a commitment to studies. Spirituality is a plus in anything you do. You need spiritual development to secure divine backing for extraordinary output. Read the stories of great men in your field. Those who walk, walk with many; those who run, run with a few; but those who fly, fly alone. You do not need more than God's vote to be anything He wants you to be. Show your leadership by taking responsibility where you are, and in so doing you will create your future. When given opportunities to serve, work not just to *be paid* but work to *be made*. The keys you acquire as you serve in different capacities will become great assets to you when your responsibilities increase.

The experience you have gained makes you who you are. Do not waste the lessons learned from them. The greater the challenge of your past, the more likely your followers are encouraged to give you a chance to prove that you are capable.

The successes you have had in the past speak volumes to your followers. It helps them understand what you can do. Work on developing your relationships with people. The deeper your relationships, the stronger your potential for leadership.

As a leader, develop your skills to manage your tasks with expertise. There is no spiritual or physical substitute for skill. Every leadership endeavor demands skill. (Psalm 78:22) As soon as your task is defined, you need to build up the required skill to accomplish it. No ministry will outgrow the quality of its structure.

Do not be satisfied to stop where you are. Celebrate the progress you have made thus far but keep growing and working on yourself to get better every day. You may have left Egypt, but since you have not yet reached your promised land, keep growing as you read and learn. You can grow in your career by learning more skills to develop your potential. You can grow in your knowledge of God, in your profession, in character development, and in every other aspect of your life. Keep moving. Do not be like a stagnant pond. Flow like a channel and be an asset instead of a liability. No one is a nonentity. We are all loaded with gifts and skills. Allow your gifts and the sweet fragrances inside you to rise and bless many. Life is about touching other lives and making an impact.

Work hard on improving yourself in every aspect of your life; physically, spiritually, financially, and academically. The room for improvement is the largest room in the world. Add value to yourself and you will become sought after. Invest in your growth as an individual to fulfill your destiny. Do not be satisfied where you are right now. There is always a better you that has not yet been attained. Aim at getting there, study more, learn more, and be versatile. Grow daily.

He Makes the Holy Spirit His Senior Partner

Leadership is not a matter of the head, but of the heart. If your heart is not attuned to the Holy Spirit, if you are not close enough to have Him fully direct your affairs, you will make a shipwreck of your leadership. (Galatians 5:24-25) When the Holy Spirit takes full control of your life, He transforms your character and your attitudes and conforms you to Christ's image. It is through the help of the Holy Spirit that you can develop a godly and righteous attitude. He works on your mind to ensure that your motives are right. He wants to make you pleasing to Himself in every area of your life. He prepares you as a leader to do your work confidently, to be dependable and trustworthy before your followers.

The Holy Spirit is the "Administrator of God's earthly estate." He is your helper, counselor, teacher, provider, and strength. In John 14:16-17, Jesus said, *"And I will pray the Father, and He will give you another Helper, that He may abide with you forever, the Spirit of truth, whom the world cannot receive, because it neither sees Him nor knows Him; but you know Him, for He dwells with you and will be in you. I will not leave you orphans; I will come to you."*

And in verse 26 he said; *"But the Helper, the Holy Spirit, whom the Father will send in My name, He will teach you all things, and bring to your remembrance all things that I said to you. "Peace I leave with you, My peace I give to you; not as the world gives do I give to you. Let not your heart be troubled, neither let it be afraid."* Hebrews 13:6 states, *"So You can boldly say, the Lord is my helper, I will not fear, what can man do to me?"* In Psalm 32:8 the Lord says, *I will instruct thee and teach thee in the way which thou shalt go: I will guide thee with mine eye.*

Get to know the Holy Spirit. He is your closest friend. He is a person, and He is always with you and dwells in you. (1 Corinthians 3:16) Let Him know that you are aware of His presence. Fall in love with Him deeply. The more you love Him, the greater your impact on earth will be. (1 Corinthians 2:9) Your impact in the Kingdom cannot exceed your love for God. Pursue and seek him with passion.

A passionate love and desire for God will keep us from sin, put a burning zeal in our hearts to study His Word, and learn His ways. It is impossible to carry out divine mandates with the arm of the flesh. The greatest waste of time is to attempt to carry out in the flesh what can be easily done by the Holy Spirit. Every great mandate or destiny needs the Holy Spirit to be accomplished.

The Holy Spirit portrays the splendor and the magnificence of one's destiny. It is He who magnifies our destiny and showcases us to the world. No one can live a successful and fruitful Christian life without Him. He makes the ride to heaven fun.

He Is Influential and Trustworthy

Leadership is influence. Leaders should know where they are going and be able to inspire and persuade others to gladly follow them. They must earn the trust and confidence of their people. People should gladly listen to you, not only because of the truth you convey, but because of their respect for you. Lead in a way that will naturally attract people to you. A quality leader does not look for followers.

He Is Sacrificial

Sacrifice is going the extra mile on a course you believe in or a goal you have vowed to reach. It is paying a special price that can give you a unique place in your field. The quality of your sacrifice will determine the level of your leadership. There is never a star without a well-defined record of sacrifice.

Great leaders are born on the altar of sacrifice. They emerge through sacrifice as pillars of rescue for their generation. Until the altar of sacrifice is prepared in a life, leadership cannot be achieved. Every player is a potential star, but not every player emerges a star until the needed price is paid. You will never find a story of outstanding success without reading about the outstanding sacrifices made. Many of us are not investing in our spiritual lives. There is a space for every one of us at the top. (Deuteronomy 8:1) If you pay the needed price, you will find yourself there.

The higher you go as a leader, the more you must give up. Until you pass the test of sacrifice, you can never emerge as a great leader. Willingness to pay the price of leadership determines how fast you get to your destiny.

There is nothing you get without paying the required price. Nothing good works out on its own; things are *made* to work if they must work. There is enough room for everyone willing to pay the price, to emerge a leader. Leadership is costly. It is not cheap talk. It's hard work.

When your life lacks a bearing, it becomes a burden. People may have seen you as a problem, but you have a responsibility to prove to them that you are a solution, an asset, and not a liability. People may have seen you as a challenge; prove to them that you are a champion. Cease to be a prayer project and a burden and be a praise project and a blessing. It is never too late to be right. Every situation can be changed. If you pay the price, you will see the result.

Chapter Six

THE MANDATES OF THE APOSTOLIC LEADER

God wants every apostolic leader to carry out certain tasks for the Kingdom. Some of these tasks are as follows.

Pray Effectual Fervent, Fiery Prayers (Acts 4:31; 6:4)

Prayer continues to be the spiritual master key to open every shut door in the spirit. The apostles taught their world to pray. They gave birth to the New Testament church in a prayer meeting in the upper room. The Holy Spirit was first received in that prayer meeting.

For the early apostles, intense prayer was the number one item on their agenda. In Acts 6:4, the apostles pledged to give themselves continually to prayers and the ministry of the Word. When they prayed, the place where they were assembled was shaken, and they were all filled with the Holy Spirit. (Acts 4:31) That is the apostolic prayer pattern. The apostles were men of prayer.

The apostolic mandate is being restored to the Church today. The prayer momentum of the season that we have entered will be stronger than what it was 10 years ago. Apostolic leaders have a mandate to bring the church back to prayer. They are to release the grace for those earth-quaking prayers.

The apostolic grace enables one to pray and sing in a way that shatters prison doors and breaks chains. Paul and Silas found themselves in prison. They began to pray apostolic prayers, and God released an earthquake of deliverance that broke their bondage and the yokes of the enemy. (Acts 16:25-40) The apostolic prayer pattern was powerful and impactful. Many prayers prayed in church today are born out of the flesh and yield no result. That which is born of the flesh is flesh, and that which is born of the spirit is spirit. No wonder we have a brand of Christians who do not hate what God hates and makes little or no impact on their world.

It was not so with the apostles. Their prayers were passionate, aggressive, pure, fiery prayers that produced immediate results. (James 5:16) They were life-quaking, situation-shaking, earth-quaking, building-quaking, and kingdom-quaking prayers. Even the physical environment and the structures housing them came under the weight of their prayers.

Their prayers carried weight in the spirit realm. After they went through Christ's tutorial on prayer, they were no longer amateurs at prayer. The effect of their prayers not only shook the spirit realm, their environment and the structures they were in were physically shaken. The result was that they became intoxicated with the Holy Spirit, and a new boldness, courage, power, and unction came upon all of them.

As apostolic leaders, we should learn to take prayer to its highest level, to enable the Church to produce the required, unprecedented, global impact in our day, that will bring in the final harvest. The apostolic prayer pattern is powerful and impactful. It addresses stubborn situations which have no choice but to bow.

Apostolic Prayers Can Do the Following
- They can embolden one. (Acts 4:13)
- They can cause prison doors and iron gates to open supernaturally. (Acts 12:1-11)
- They can empower you to advance beyond any opposition in your way. (1 Corinthians 15:9)
- They can produce earthquakes of deliverance and usher many souls into the Kingdom. (Acts 16:25-40)

- They can accelerate your progress in life and ministry. (Acts 6:7)
- They can release you into your full potential and calling. (Acts 13:2)
- They can get God's attention. (John 20:10-18)

As apostolic leaders reintroduce passionate, fiery prayer to the church today, it will speed the rate at which prayers are answered. Very soon, prayers that typically took a week, a month, or a year to be answered, will receive immediate attention.

Release the Spirit of Repentance Upon The Church

Repentance is a key to unlock the heavens, get God's attention, and bring God into our situations. It opens five important doors: the doors of mercy, grace, forgiveness, reconciliation, and restoration. It is one way of suspending the devastation caused by sin and the activities of the evil one. Apostolic leaders will lead the Church into quality repentance at individual, family, community, national and international levels, so that lingering generational curses may be totally broken.

As we, His Church repents, we invite Him into our circumstances to terminate the things that have held us in bondage and strangulated our progress toward our destiny. He will remove them and, in their place, usher in times of refreshing and a restoration of all things. (Act 3:18-20)

Restore Quality Praise and Worship to The Church

The intensity of true worship will increase as apostolic leaders release that concept in the Church. If God's glory will be ushered back into His temple in this era, it will not be without praise and worship. The Church will learn to sing prophetic songs that will touch hearts and change lives. Their worship will not sound like empty noise to the Lord. They will not sing and worship in the flesh or from the lips, but in spirit and in truth. Their worship will move Him to minister back to His body. He will be moved to rejoice over them with gladness, dancing, and singing. (Zephaniah 3:17; Acts 16:25)

In Acts 13:2-4, as the disciples in Antioch began to minister to the Lord with pure hearts in one accord through praise and worship, the Holy Spirit came down in His power to enjoy their worship and to give them instructions. In this Kingdom age, we must learn to praise God always and allow His praise to be continually on our lips. The Church cannot afford to move without being clearly instructed by their Commander, the Holy Spirit. Praise and worship are major avenues through which He comes to dish out such instructions. If the glory of God is to be ushered back into His sanctuary, then we must provide the chariot to bring it back, and that chariot is Praise and Worship.

Stand for Holiness

Uncovering and judging sin are the responsibility of the Church. It's time for iniquity to be exposed and for judgment to be meted out quickly. I recently heard of two incidents that took place in Pentecostal churches. One involved an elder in a large Pentecostal church, while the other one involved a pastor. The two men died on top of mistresses they had been living with, in immorality. Only God knows how long they had been living in adultery. Unknown to them, we have entered a new season, they were judged in the very act.

This is a serious season for the Church. It will expose, rebuke and judge sin and unrighteousness. The purity and strength of the early church will be fully restored. The days of Ananias and Sapphira are returning to the Church. Note that Sapphira died, not necessarily because she told lies like her husband, but because of her lateness to church. She arrived three hours after the husband died. Maybe she was busy dressing and putting on her makeup. If she had been there on time and had seen what happened to him when he lied, she would have spoken the truth and been spared. But because she was a late and did not know what had transpired before she came, she fell into the same trap. She told the same lie and died on the spot.

These are the days when God should not be mocked; when His forbearance should not be taken for weakness; and when judgment is being released against iniquity faster than before. These are days when the sins that will send many to hell will not be "big, known sins" like fornication and adultery, but presumptuous sins of the heart which could easily be viewed as things that do not matter. A stronger manifestation of the gifts of the Holy Spirit will ensure that hidden sins are exposed. No wonder David prayed that God would deliver him from presumptuous sins. Personal, business, marital and ministry foundations are being tried and exposed today.

Activate Apostolic Graces Upon Many

Acts 4:33 made it clear that the apostles witnessed about the resurrection of the Lord Jesus with power, and great grace was upon them all. The apostles, full of grace, were able to rule their world without struggling. As an apostolic leader, you must be full of grace and be able to activate grace in the lives of many around you. Stir up grace in your life as you pray and study His Word. (2 Timothy 1:6) It is only received in His presence. Grace is God's unmerited favor and divine enablement to do extraordinary things that ordinary men cannot do. Grace is divine enablement. It is what makes a natural man supernatural and an ordinary man, extraordinary.

Grace is "the God factor" that enables you to win and live your life without struggling. Without God's gracious favor, we cannot live victoriously. But when we attract His favor, we become a pleasure to Him. He can look at us and smile.

Grace turns nobodies into celebrities, qualifies the disqualified and distinguishes the despised. It enables you to outrun those that have gone ahead of you. It pulls those at the bottom up to the top. It introduces the most unlikely candidates. It causes the tolerated to be celebrated. Grace may bring you into positions for which you are not yet fully qualified and stand you before many. It connects you to those who matter, lifts and introduces you to the world.

Grace enables you to perform beyond the expectations of men and equips you to outrun and overtake those that have gone ahead of you. Grace covers your errors and colors your effort.

War Against the Powers Fighting the Church

The apostles were militant, strong and hardworking people, not a lazy crowd. They ran to win. They were warriors who took the battle to the gates of the enemy. The apostles taught and practiced spiritual warfare. Many of the Scripture passages we use in spiritual warfare training were given to us by the apostles. They were great warriors. (2 Corinthians 10:3-6; Ephesians 6:12)

Paul, a warrior, trained the Church in Ephesus in battle. As a result, they subdued the evil goddess of Diana, the demonic ruler of the continent of Asia, which ushered in the longest lasting revival in history.

Apostolic leaders have a mandate to confront the menacing forces of darkness over states and nations. They confront and conquer new territories with military precision. Today's Church is not to be a defensive, but an offensive Church that will occupy until the Master comes. We are to fight with the Word to ensure that the enemy is put on the run every day.

We are to identify things that have hindered God's move and His manifest presence in His Church in time past and be ready to pay whatever price necessary to usher Him back to His sanctuary. Christ Himself is the Commander-in-Chief of God's Kingdom army. Wherever He is, there is victory. A warring Church is emerging today that will go back where she lost ground to the enemy in the times past and recover her victory.

Had it been possible for the devil to stop the apostles, he would be able to stop us. But since he could not stop them, despite all his threats, he cannot stop us. Even death could not stop them. Read the confession of the Apostle Paul in Acts 20:22-24. They were not stopped by evil plots and harassment, death, sin, compromise, or lack of resources.

> *"And see, now I go bound in the spirit to Jerusalem, not knowing the things that will happen to me there, 'except that the Holy Spirit testifies in every city, saying that chains and tribulations await me.' But none of these things move me; nor do I count my life dear to myself, so that I may finish my race with joy and the ministry which I received from the Lord Jesus, to testify to the gospel of the grace of God."*

Nothing could separate them from the love of God in Christ Jesus. (Romans 8:35-38) They were good fighters and finishers and arrived in heaven as Generals. In 2 Timothy 4:7-8, Paul testified of himself, saying, *"I have fought a good fight, I have finished my course, I have kept the faith."* As apostolic leaders, we will finish the great work those apostles began.

God will use us as His battle axes to deal with kingdoms, empires, and armies. (Jeremiah 51:20-22) We are a confrontational army, raised to confront sin and the devil, first in our own lives and then in the lives of others in the church, and in the nations. We are God's instruments who will not only defend our territories but will carry the battles to the gates of the enemy. (Isaiah 28:6) We will confront the strongmen and deliver their captives. (Isaiah 49:24-26) Every part of our body is a weapon of warfare and we will operate as a secret army. As we invade the enemy's camp, we wreak havoc in his kingdom.

God is putting the spirit of the Lion of the Tribe of Judah in us to confront wickedness wherever we encounter it. "Sacred cows" will be confronted. Apostolic leaders will operate with the boldness of prophets and speak God's mind and counsel without fear or favor. Their messages will not be sugar coated. They will not mince words. (Acts 13:19) They will confront with authority because they know who sent them. They have been called to set the captives free, loose them from their bondage, give sight to the blind and declare jubilee for the Church. (Luke 4:18) No time will be given negotiating with the devil or being intimidated by him. They must execute God's vengeance over him. (Psalms 149:6-9) They will terrorize the kingdom of darkness. They are a formidable and committed army that recovers lost ground. As they confront, they conquer new ground and recover the Church's inheritance.

Diligently Carry Out Kingdom Assignments

Apostles are strong and hardworking people, not a sleeping and lazy bunch. They run to finish. They have special strength from the Lord soar above the mountains and the storms of life.

We apostolic leaders need to be conscious of the fact that the harvest is plenteous, but the laborers are few. God, Himself is ready to take as many as can move with Him into the field. It is a season of quick work. He will do a quick work and will need men who are spiritually alert, who have an accurate understanding of the times, and know what must be done. Get busy for God. It is better to pour out all that God has given you and die empty than to sit and die full.

We must work hard to maximize our potential if we are to change the world. We cannot be lazy and work at maximum potential at the same time. Whatever the bottlenecks may be, stay on it till you accomplish your goal. The fact that you are experiencing some difficulties along the way in carrying out your purpose does not mean God is not in it.

Paul was a hard worker. He said in Acts 20:33-35:

"I have coveted no man's silver, or gold, or apparel. Yea, ye yourselves know, that these hands have ministered unto my necessities, and to them that were with me. I have shewed you all things, how that so laboring ye ought to support the weak, and to remember the words of the Lord Jesus, how he said, It is more blessed to give than to receive."

In Colossians 3:23 we read: *"And whatsoever ye do, do it heartily, as to the Lord, and not unto men; knowing that of the Lord ye shall receive the reward of the inheritance: for ye serve the Lord Christ."*

Boldly Stand for God Through Thick and Thin

The boldness of the apostles was so outstanding that it confused those who opposed them. They were not intimidated by threats or persecution. *"When they saw the boldness of Peter and John, and perceived that they were uneducated and untrained men, they marveled. And they realized they had been with Jesus"* (Acts 4:13). Notice that when the apostles were threatened and opposed, they never asked God to stop their opposition. They understood that it was part of the package for their task.

Instead, they asked Him to *"... grant to your servants that, with all boldness, they may speak your word"* (Acts 4:29). In Acts 14:3, we are told that they spoke boldly in the Lord, which gave testimony unto the Word of His grace, and granted signs and wonders to be done by their hands.

They had a mandate to obey God rather than men and were ready to lay down their lives for the cause they believed in. They boldly asked the religious leaders who threatened to kill them to judge among themselves if it was not better to obey God rather than men. (Acts 5:29)

Boldness is a hallmark of apostolic leaders. Boldness has to do with refusing every form of intimidation, but instead, being courageous, blunt and outspoken. You cannot be with Jesus and remain a coward. No tiger bears a feeble cub. We must exhibit the boldness of the Lion of the tribe of Judah. We need boldness to carry out the exploits of this Kingdom age. Our assignments may involve going to see kings on their thrones and confronting the gates of hell.

We have a mandate to root out sin, religiosity and to pull down the strongholds of the enemy. We will not be dismayed or intimidated by the threats of the wicked. We must execute God's vengeance over His enemies and pronounce on them the judgments written. Without boldness, we cannot carry out these assignments.

Exercise Apostolic Faith

The apostles of old were people whose fiery faith could not be put out by the chilly waters of persecution. They were full of faith and were able to carry out great exploits.

In Acts 3, we have the incident of the man who had been lame from birth, for more than 40 years. The apostles were on fire from home and going to the prayer meeting to get more fire. On the way, a crippled beggar who had been there and had received alms from several people met them and requested alms. But they said, *"We do not have money here with us, but we have something more precious to give you than money. In the name of Jesus, rise up and walk."*

The man looked at them and wondered if they had even noticed his crippled situation. He sat at the Beautiful Gate, and yet he could not get into the temple. That is a very frustrating situation. He could hear the melodies coming out of the sanctuary and see men and women walk in and out through the gate to enjoy fellowship with God, but he could not. These two men come by insulting his condition by asking him to get up and walk. Could they not see he was crippled? He didn't realize that he was about to have the shock of his life.

Peter said to him, "I am not here to discuss this with you. The anointing of God is not on me for a decoration." They laid their hands on the man, and their faith sent strength to his legs, which stretched out by force. Of course, the man immediately got up and began to jump, leap and praise God, which was a demonstration of faith.

In Acts 6:8-10 Stephen, full of faith and power, did great wonders and miracles among the people. These early apostles were able to carry out exploits for the Kingdom by faith. They did not see situations with physical eyes, but with the eyes of faith. To them, no task was impossible. They spoke faith-filled words over situations. Their faith was dynamic, active and unstoppable. It won all their battles and never wavered regardless of the obstacles that appeared. They believed the impossible and caused the natural to give way to the supernatural. They were not moved by sight, but by the Word of God. Their rugged faith intimidated the devil. It transformed situations like the healing of the crippled man at the beautiful gate.

The apostles had a positive attitude toward life. Despite the challenges they faced, they continued to rejoice in their persecution and held steadfastly to their confession. For them, joy was not the absence of challenges, it was the presence of God in the midst of them. They continued singing and praising God through it all. Even amidst the fire, they continued to praise and glorify the Lord. They never saw the bigness of their problems or challenges because they were conscious of the greatness of their God. They praised God, even in the worst situations.

Apostolic leaders should see with eyes of faith and understand the power of positivity. For without faith, it is impossible to please God, For He who comes to God must believe that He is and that He is a rewarder of them that diligently seek him. (Hebrews 11:6) Even when you are confronted with a very challenging situation, refuse to see it with ordinary eyes. See God's ability in your inabilities and refuse to be defeated in your thoughts and confessions. Refuse defeat. See yourself as a giant over your situation, and you will surely conquer. You need the kind of faith the apostles had to be able to face the challenges staring at you. You need faith that sees the possibility of victory in every challenge and believes God's Word in the face of contradictory circumstances.

See no mountain as insurmountable. It is only by faith that you can handle impossible situations, bulldoze through impossible places and emerge unhurt. Faith initiates your victory even before the battle begins and propels you to that victory in the physical. You cannot deny the existence of giants, but you can conquer them by fixing your gaze on God. No matter how insurmountable your giants may appear, they cannot be compared to our God who has already given us victory over them.

Aggressively Preach the Gospel

The apostles were aggressive evangelists. They preached the Word in season and out of season. They saw it as their obligation to preach the gospel, and they did it passionately. Paul said in 1 Corinthians 9:16, *"For if I preach the gospel, I have nothing to boast of, for necessity is laid upon me; yes, woe is me if I do not preach the gospel!"*

Their commission in Acts 1:8 was to preach the gospel in Jerusalem, Judea, Samaria and the uttermost parts of the earth. Paul said in 2 Corinthians 5:11, *"Knowing, therefore, the terror of the Lord, we persuade men; but we are well known to God, and I also trust are well known in your consciences."*

Acts 6:4, 7, *"And will give our attention to prayer and the ministry of the word." And the word of God increased; and the number of the disciples multiplied in Jerusalem greatly, and a great company of the priests were obedient to the faith."*

The great commission God has given us must not become the great omission. As apostolic leaders, we need to give evangelism its rightful place. So much emphasis will be laid on aggressive prophetic evangelism. Believers will receive new strategies to win the lost. The Church will again realize that evangelism is their greatest commission and will not make it the great omission. The zeal for evangelism will overtake many. It is a season of aggressive evangelism. A force which people cannot control will propel many to wake up from their complacency and slumber and move into the field of evangelism and missions. (Psalm 68:11)

A great company has emerged around the world to publish the Word. We are part of that company that will trumpet for God through morning cries, preaching in buses, passing out tracts, market evangelism. Open-air crusades will regain momentum. This is the season of the great harvest of souls. More emphasis will be placed on evangelism; more mission agencies will arise as the Church begins to get more conscious of missions.

People will come under great convictions of their sins and seek to be saved. The Church will begin to shun sin and unrighteousness as never before. Many will be set free from spiritual bondage. Drama ministries will increase, and many Christian actors will arise to evangelize the world through this medium.

Faith commences your victory

Different ways to preach the gospel as the opportunities offer themselves.

- Reach out with your own life. Let it be an epistle that men will read and find Jesus.
- Reach out to those in the hospitals and pray for them.

- Reach out to those in the prisons and release deliverance to the captives.
- Reach out to the schools; pupil, students and teachers or lecturers.
- Reach out by organizing tea parties in your home or open-air outings in your neighborhood.
- Preach the Word of God on buses and distribute tracts.
- Carry out evangelistic crusades as God enables you.
- Embark on preaching God's Word early in the morning and evening with a megaphone.
- Have prayer feasts in your home and invite others.
- Use your birthday or anniversary celebrations to preach the gospel.
- Visit the prisons and the hospitals to minister and recover God's apostles and evangelists there.
- Visit the brothels and hotels too.

Pioneer, Pathfinder, and Pacesetter for Kingdom Projects.

The apostolic Church was a pioneering and pacesetting Church. Apostles initiated moves and efforts that pushed the global Church forward. They kept her on the cutting edge where she influenced what happened in her environment. Acts 17:6 states that they turned their world upside down. The apostolic grace made them trailblazers, pathfinders, forerunners, initiators, and "establishers." They dared the impossible. They broke through seemingly impossible situations with boldness to open the nations to the gospel and to God's agenda for them.

They penetrated areas that other people had difficulties getting into and ushered the light of the gospel into them. They invaded new territories, confronted powers of darkness in those territories, subdued them and brought them under the leadership of God. Paul dealt with idolatry in Athens and introduced them to the true God whom they did not know. He fought with beasts at Ephesus, confronted Diana of the Ephesians and persuaded many to turn from the worship of idols to worship the true God.

The apostles were the agents of change. Whenever God wants to bring about a remarkable change in the New Testament Church, He introduced strong apostolic grace to facilitate it. Apostolic leaders are change agents. We are to be in the forefront where we can create the events that others watch and make the news that others listen to. Like the daughters of Zelophehad in Numbers 27:1-11, we should initiate new things. Like Elizabeth in Luke 1:60, we should stand against things we do not agree with without being intimidated. We must lead the way in making a difference in our world.

Carry and Distribute God's Fire Everywhere You Go.

"And there appeared unto them cloven tongues like as of fire, and it sat upon each of them" (Acts 2:3).

On the day of Pentecost, when the Holy Spirit descended upon the apostles and released tongues of fire on each of them, they were changed from inside out. The fire transformed them into firebrands. Their tongues caught fire and their boldness increased. The fire was burning so hot in their bones that they could not contain it. It was under the influence of that fire that Peter, a fisherman preached, and 3,000 souls gave their lives to Jesus on one day. We need that fire. As His firebrands, we should distribute this fire wherever we go. (Psalms 104:4)

In Matthew 3:11, John said,

"I indeed baptize you with water unto repentance, but He who is coming after me is mightier than I, whose sandals I am not worthy to carry. He will baptize you with the Holy Spirit and fire."

Jesus said in Luke 12:49 that He came to set fire on the earth. As apostolic leaders, we should be fire carriers. God's fire burning in our bones should consume the camp of the wicked. It should cleanse us and those around us. It should burn off the impurities in our lives and leave us like pure gold. It should consume every ounce of pride and anything else God did not plant in our lives, homes, churches and in the nations. It should kindle a new zeal and passion for God in our hearts. It should burn away faulty foundations and lay for us a new and solid foundation.

It should make us Holy Ghost law enforcement agents to set things in order and re-align them according to God's will. This fire will empower and embolden us to challenge the devil. It should make us too hot for any demon from hell to touch. It will make us terrors to hell and keep us bubbling forth in the spirit. Through thick and thin, we remain strong because His fire is burning in our bones. Nothing discourages us. We can advance the cause of the Kingdom and bring liberation to many.

Be A Kingdom Financier and Mobilizer – Luke 8:1-3

During Jesus' earthly ministry, a group of leaders worked with and supported Him. In Luke 8:3, we are told that they were an invaluable financial resource for Jesus' ministry.

God has ordained that wealth will change hands in this Kingdom age, from the hands of unbelievers to the hands of the saints. The riches of the Gentiles will be put into our hands for our Father is the One who gives power to create wealth. (Deuteronomy 8:18; Isaiah 61:6b) God gives us the treasures of darkness and the hidden riches of secret places. (Isaiah 45:3) He brings to us the abundance of the seas and heaps for us gold as dust and gives us plenty of silver. (Isaiah 60:5; Job 22:24-25)

Today, God is looking for Kingdom financiers, who will see themselves as stewards of God's money and will be good accountants of the wealth that will be entrusted into their hands. Wealth will also change hands from believers who use it for self-aggrandizement to the hands of those who will use it to serve the interests of the Kingdom. These financiers will have large Kingdom hearts which will enable them to see things from a Kingdom perspective. They will gladly serve the church, not their own agenda, with the resources God puts into their hands.

As apostolic leaders, we will learn absolute dependence on the Lord for all that is needed. We will not depend on men; neither will we use gimmicks to raise money. There will be a fuller understanding that if God owns a work, He supports it. The Church will learn to consult Him each time they have a need.

Heaven's company is unlimited. The Church must have faith in God's divine provision. Our responsibility is to inform Him when we run out of supplies. The earth is the Lord's and the fullness thereof. Distance cannot limit Him. Silver and gold are His. The cattle on a thousand hills belong to Him.

Live by And Teach God's Word

The early apostles made up their minds to give time to prayer and the study of the Word. It was their priority. *"But we will give ourselves continually to prayer and to the ministry of the Word."* (Acts 6:4) They went from house to house to fellowship and study the Word together.

God's Word guides, inspires and equips us for relevance in our day. That is why Joshua was instructed to build and operate his life on God's Word if he wanted to successfully reach his destiny. (Joshua 1:8-9)

Psalms 1:1-3 also confirms this.

> *"Blessed is the man that walketh not in the counsel of the ungodly, nor standeth in the way of sinners, nor sitteth in the seat of the scornful. But his delight is in the law of the LORD, and in his law doth he meditate day and night. And he shall be like a tree planted by the rivers of water, that bringeth forth his fruit in his season; his leaf also shall not wither, and whatsoever he doeth shall prosper."*

The more we delight in His Word, the more we will receive the spiritual nourishment we need to bear fruit at the right season. As we discover our potential and position ourselves where we can meet needs around us, we become a sought-after planting of the Lord, to showcase His glory.

No believer can survive and be effective without adequate knowledge of God's Word. God's word is creative, sharp, effective and powerful. It is Life. It is our mirror. It sharpens and builds up. All that we need to prosper in life is found in the word.

As an apostolic leader, you need to cultivate a habit of spending time daily studying and meditating God's Word. His Word fuels every prayer to become effective. Your "Word-level" determines your prayer level. Do not just read His Word, study it, meditate on it, and apply it. (Colossians 3:16; Joshua 1:8) As you speak the Word and meditate on it, it will make you prosperous and give you good success.

As apostolic leaders, we ought to meditate on His Word as we fellowship with the Spirit of truth. We get to know His voice as we read His Word. It is a messenger and runs swiftly to accomplish His will. God hastens after His Word to perform it. (Jeremiah 1:12) His Word is a cleanser and a purifier. It is the refiner's fire and the fuller's soap. It will lift you from spiritual weakling to a militant, mature firebrand Christian, too tough for the devil to mess around with.

God's Word provides wisdom and understanding, and deeper revelations. It saves us from errors and misconceptions. It is a pillar to lean on and delivers us from unnecessary struggle. It is a corrective measure. It helps us achieve our purpose in life. It is effective, powerful and creative. It is the beginning and the end of everything. It is our mirror. Read it daily.

Model What You Preach

As an apostolic leader, you should have good reputation. Your life should be a living epistle of what you preach, so you can boldly ask your followers to imitate you. (1 Corinthians 11:1)

God's Word tells us that we have been made a kingdom of priests and kings, to build and advance his kingdom on earth. (Revelation 1:5-6) We are a chosen generation, a royal priesthood, a holy nation, a peculiar people, born to show forth the praises of Him who has called us out of darkness into his marvelous light. (1 Peter 2:9)

We are to fulfill God's mandate and advance His Kingdom in the marketplace. The marketplace is our parish, a harvest field and an extension of God's Kingdom, not just a place to make money. It is a strategic place where you meet all kinds of people who need help, who want their lives and destinies transformed.

Who Are You?

- You are His Light to lighten the dark world, you are a city set on the hill that cannot be hidden but meant to provide light to everyone in darkness. Let your light so shine before men that they may see your good works and give God glory. (Matthew 5:14-16)
- You should shine forth as light wherever you are, and the darkness will not comprehend your light. (John 1: 4-5)
- Brighten every dark corner where you are by shining forth his glory through your life. (Isaiah 60:1)
- You are His epistle, meant to be read by all men. (2 Corinthians 3:2)
- You are His fragrance, expected to swallow the foul smell of sin everywhere. (2 Corinthians 2:15)
- You are His representative, His ambassador. (2 Corinthians 5:20)
- People must see the beauty of Jesus in your life and know you by the fruit you bear. (Matthew 7:16)
- You are the salt of the earth, meant to season the tasteless world, to preserve her from decay and to bring healing to her putrefying sores. (Matthew 5: 13)

Apostolic leader, God is sending us into the marketplace to showcase Him to our world. The church building is a training ground and a place for the equipping of the saints. Real ministry is found outside the church building where the sinners are. You are His image maker and billboard out there. You need to reflect His character and power both in your home, church and in the marketplace. You are to bring financial dividends into the kingdom through whatever you do for a living. That is what the apostolic anointing is about, that is how to occupy till He comes. You are a change agent in the marketplace. But to be a change agent, you must first be a changed agent.

As Jesus went about doing good, touching lives, delivering the oppressed, healing the sick and leaving people better than He found them, so must we. We are extensions of His arms to help the needy, to encourage the brokenhearted, and show them the path of life.

Confront and Expose Evil

Apostolic leaders are part of the "Not So Company" that God is raising up who will boldly speak out to correct issues in their generation. In Luke 1:60, Elizabeth, an apostolic leader of her time was a woman of the spirit. She knew the mind of God concerning her son John. Because of the encounter her husband had in the temple that made him dumb, he could not name his baby. His relatives chose to call him "Zechariah junior" after his father. But Elizabeth arose as a "not so mother." His name shall be John.

"Not so leaders" are still in high demand today as iniquity is abounding in the church and the world. Prostitution, same-sex marriage, terrorism, abortion, violence and many other vices are staring us in the face. Where are the "Not So Apostolic Leaders" who will arise and confront these evils? God is putting the Spirit of the Lion of the Tribe of Judah in us to confront wickedness wherever we find it. Apostolic leaders will operate with the boldness of prophets and speak God's mind and counsel without fear or favor. Their messages will not be sugar-coated, nor will they mince words. (Acts 13:19)

They will confront with authority because they know the One who sent them. They have been called to set captives free, loose bonds, give sight to the blind and declare jubilee for the Church. (Luke 4:18) They will neither negotiate with the devil nor be intimidated by him.

They will execute God's vengeance over him. (Psalms 149:6-9) They will terrorize the kingdom of darkness.

Showcase His Power to Your Generation

The decade 2011-2020 will be the most powerful decade in history for the global church. God will be reintroduced to the world with uncommon supernatural signs, wonders, and miracles. It is a decade of evidence, and proof producers. Apostolic leaders are called to reactivate and demonstrate a higher apostolic grace, authority, and anointing if the global Church is to recover lost ground and finish strong.

The apostles' preaching of the Word came with great power as they testified to Jesus' resurrection. (Acts 4:33) They did not make any effort to introduce themselves. Their works spoke more volumes than their words. Their preaching of the Word was accompanied by notable signs and wonders. (Acts 4:16) Through the apostles, perfect soundness was restored to the sick. (Acts 3:16) Fear came upon every soul: and many wonders and signs were done by the apostles. (Acts 2:43) The apostles gave powerful witness of the resurrection of the Lord Jesus, and great grace was upon them all. (Acts 4:33)

People, like Paul, were not only known for polished grammar and eloquence, but also for demonstrations of God's power, which they performed. (1 Corinthians 2:4-5) It was through signs and wonders, by the power of the Spirit of God, that Paul preached the gospel. (Romans 15:19) No wonder so many lives were touched and impacted through his life and ministry.

In 2 Corinthians 12:12, Paul said, *"The signs of an apostle were wrought among you in all patience, in signs and wonders and mighty deeds."* In Acts 19:11–12, God wrought special miracles through Paul, so that many were healed simply by his apron. Apostolic leaders need to manifest this kind of anointing today. It acquired only by spending quality time with the Lord in the closet, seeking His face, studying His word, and praying in the Holy Ghost.

The power and glory of God are reserved for hungry and thirsty people. If you are not interested, you will never see it made manifest in your life and ministry. What is not your decision will never be your destination. The hungrier you get, the stronger you become in God. If you remain hungry, the oil of God on your life will continue to flow. (2 Kings 4)

Anyone who is satisfied with where they are in the Lord will stop pursuing Him for more. When you come to a point where you are so full of God's anointing on your life that you feel that you do not need more of Him, you'll be sidelined. God is interested in empty vessels, not the ones that are full. The widow was asked to set aside any container that was full. She kept pouring until she got to a point where there were no more vessels to be filled, and the oil stopped flowing. The flow of the oil continues as long as there are vessels to contain it. Once the vessels need no more oil, the flow will cease.

The oil is only for empty vessels. To stir up this hunger, you must see your helplessness and your dire need for Him. It guarantees the flow of the spirit. If you feel you are powerful, strong and self-sufficient, you have excused yourself from the strength of the Spirit and have become Holy Spirit deficient. Your sufficiency is of God. (2 Corinthians 3:5) He makes His strength available to those who know that they have nothing to offer outside of Him, those who realize their helplessness and nothingness without Him. You must come to the end of yourself before you can begin with God. (2 Corinthians 12:9) His strength is made perfect in our weakness.

Partner Closely with The Holy Spirit.

If you are full of the Spirit, your words will prick the hearts of men. Because the early apostle's words were filled with the Holy Spirit, they achieved the results they needed each time they spoke. (Acts 4:8)

They released the Holy Spirit everywhere they went. Stephen was full of the Holy Ghost. In Acts 7:55 we read, *"But he, being full of the Holy Ghost, looked up steadfastly into heaven, and saw the glory of God and Jesus standing at the right hand of God."*

"And God, which knoweth the hearts, bare them, witness, giving them the Holy Ghost, even as he did unto us. And put no difference between them and us, purifying their hearts by faith" (Acts 15:8-9).

Leadership is not about trusting in your natural abilities, but in submitting them to the Holy Spirit and allowing Him to use them to bless others. Every good leader seeks responsibility, not authority, but as you humbly fulfill your task, God releases on you the authority you need as a leader.

The Apostles enjoyed the comfort of the Holy Spirit! They befriended Him and allowed Him to pioneer their affairs. They were friends with the Holy Spirit. In John 14:26 He said, *"But the Helper, the Holy Spirit, whom the Father will send in My name, He will teach you all things and bring to your remembrance all things that I said to you."* (Hebrews 13:6)

You too can boldly say, "the Lord is my helper, I will not fear, what can man do to me?" The Holy Spirit leads us into the will of God. This is why we must cultivate an intimate relationship with Him. Commune and fellowship with the Holy Spirit if you wish to enter the depths of God's will.

Ephesians 5:18 encourages us to do so:

And do not be drunk with wine, in which is dissipation; but be filled with the Spirit, speaking to one another in psalms and hymns and spiritual songs, singing and making melody in your heart to the Lord, giving thanks always for all things to God the Father in the name of our Lord Jesus

Get to know the Holy Spirit. He is your closest friend, who is always with you. You are the temple in which He lives. (1 Corinthians 3:16) Be continually conscious of His presence. Fall in love with Him, pursue and seek Him passionately. Love Him dearly and let Him make your life worth living. The more you love Him, the greater your impact will be. (1 Corinthians 2:9) Every anointed person is a lover of God. (Proverbs 21:20) A deep desire for Him will keep you from sin, give you a burning zeal to study His Word, and to learn His ways.

It is impossible to carry out divine mandates with the arm of the flesh. The greatest time waster I know is to attempt to carry out in the flesh what can be easily and correctly done by the Spirit. Even if clear and glorious and is meant to turn the whole world around or keep them at a standstill, you cannot complete that mandate if you are not endued with the Holy Spirit's power. Without His anointing, you will make a shipwreck of that vision. The Holy Spirit is the one who magnifies our destiny and displays us to the world. Whatever we achieve without Him is as dung. He gives meaning to life and makes our ride to heaven enjoyable.

To Encourage the Church To Go Back To Missions

The apostles of old were on the move, traversing through many lands, conquering new worlds. They were not idle people. Yet they were not rolling stones. They were good finishers. They made sure a major work was completed in a place before they moved to the next.

In Acts 1:8 Jesus made it clear to the apostles their primary assignment.

> *"But you shall receive power when the Holy Spirit has come upon you, and you shall be witnesses to me both in Jerusalem and in all Judea and Samaria and to the ends of the earth."*

As an apostolic leader, be conscious of the fact that the harvest is plenteous, but the laborers are few. God is ready to take as many as can move with Him into the field. It is a season of quick work.

You have a major task to restore evangelism and missions to its original pivotal position in the Church. God sent His Son as a missionary to the world to save her. He did His job and, afterward, He set up a missionary Church to finish the unfinished task. That is why in John 20:21 Jesus said, *"As the father has sent me, I also send you."*

Help the Church Work As A Team

Apostolic leaders should reflect the epitome of unconditional love and unity. Unity empowers the Church to stand against the enemy and carry out God's agenda. The enemy can easily thwart the purposes of God if he discovers that the Church is not united. In this Kingdom age, the walls of partition between us in the body of Christ will be broken down.

None will say, "I am a Greek and not a Jew." Though tribes and tongues will differ, and cultures may not be the same, unity of heart and purpose will be paramount in the Church in this era. Denominations will still exist for identity, administration, and resourcing, but the Church will not survive on simply a denominational platform. No matter how big the denomination is, it cannot stand in for the global Church or even the Church in a nation.

Since we are all of one Kingdom, going to the same heaven, we must receive that revelation of unity. There should be no room for segregation. Jesus had a dream team in mind as He prayed His last prayers on earth, *"that they may be one."* The Church in this era will be the answer to that prayer.

Apostolic leaders should focus on and emphasize issues that unite us and de-emphasize things that divide us in this Kingdom age. The sooner we accommodate one another, the better.

Apostolic leaders will be thoroughly taught and equipped so that they will teach and equip others to render to God-quality services. The gifts of the Spirit will be fully manifested in the church in this era. The body will be fed by what every joint supplies.

God will cause the prayer Jesus prayed that His church should be one, to be answered, for in unity will be our strength. Jesus worked with His disciples as a team and equally desires in this Kingdom age to see us work that way. We are not building our private companies, we are building His church. People will see themselves as stewards and custodians of whatever riches God entrusts into their hands for the purpose of the Kingdom and ensure that the needs of the Kingdom are met. Everyone's gifts and roles will be appreciated and used to serve the interests of the Kingdom.

Raise Informed Ambassadors for Heaven

Apostolic leaders have an assignment to raise diplomats for heaven who can issue orders and make decrees on behalf of heaven, men who are ambassadors of Christ, who not only make decrees but also enforce Kingdom behavior and holiness.

As ambassadors, we are to exercise delegated authority with spiritual and physical diplomatic immunity. (2 Corinthians 5:20) Our voices should be recognized in heaven and in hell. Hell should tremble when our names are mentioned. We are to intimidate the devil, not be intimidated by him. We are also to act as God's spokesmen on earth, receiving and speaking whatever new revelations God has for His people.

We are the governing body in the church that defends, directs, trains, motivates, and sustains her to her destiny. (Titus 1:5) We are the indispensable heart, the nucleus, and the centerpiece of the Church. We set the tempo and tone of every other thing that happens in the Church. The early apostles received deep divine revelation, yet they were careful not to be puffed up by it or use it for selfish gain. They used it to enrich the Body of Christ and help them to know what the Spirit was saying to the churches.

If the church does not know the mind of God, it will gradually become irrelevant both to God and to humanity. In this Kingdom age, the Holy Spirit will reveal God's heartbeat to every child of God who desires to know it.

Chapter Seven

LEADERS: ROLE MODELS AND MENTORS

A role model is a mentor, a trusted guide, counselor, and coach. He is an experienced, trusted friend and adviser who helps you to complete your calling in life. He facilitates the fulfillment of destinies. He helps you get to where you may never have arrived at on your own. Without a role model, you are slowed down and could be frustrated and limited in attaining of your destiny in life. A role model sees the potential and undeveloped gifts in a protégé and assists him in the development of his potential in life and ministry.

Role models know that they are already shinning stars in their generation, but do not stop there. They desire to make stars out of others. Their joy is to see many stars emerge because of their tutelage; stars that shine brighter than themselves. The more they mentor those who look up to them, the more they equip them to stand on their own and become more useful in the ministry.

A role model aims at improving the situation of the people he mentors, even to his own detriment at times. He is willing to provide his shoulders for them to stand on, and feathers to enable them to fly to heights that they may not have otherwise reached.

He is careful not set himself up as an idol to infer that they cannot do without him. He teaches them to lean on Jesus, not himself. He is also willing to learn from his mentee and does not present himself as someone who knows-it-all or has it all together.

He not only shares the progress he has made in life but also shares his mistakes and failures, and lessons he's learned. That way the mentee can learn from them and not repeat the same mistakes.

He models a lifestyle his mentees can emulate. If his lifestyle is one that causes no one to want to be like him, something is wrong with his modeling. Whatever you expect from people, you must first model for them.

Role models are the ladders we climb to the top. Without rungs on the ladder, there's no way to climb. Without fathers, no feathers, without feathers, you cannot fly. God is the author of the role model principle. He believes in and demonstrates fatherhood. It would be risky to start flying without having someone to pick us up if we crash. We need leaders, destiny helpers, visionary fathers who can help us complete our vision. A role model is the builder of our capacity. If we want to get anywhere quickly, we should identify a mentor. If we want to see further, it is done by standing on the shoulders of those who have gone ahead of us.

Only disciples will ever qualify to become apostles. Anyone who is not a follower is not worthy to be followed. No matter how intelligent you are, your access to the top is limited if you do not have a mentor. Role models are facilitators of destiny.

The outcome of mentoring influences productivity in life, business, and ministry. Mentorship can be carried out from a distance or at a very close range. From a distance, you can mentor someone through your books, tapes, biographies, messages on television, in conferences, or seminars. At close range, you can talk with the person, feel his heartbeat, and get his opinion on different issues and share your own heartbeat with him.

If you have a mentor whom you diligently pursue and follow, you will not only tap from the grace of God in that person's life, but you will have what it takes to double accomplishments. Mentees can carry a double portion of the anointing of their mentors while their mentors are still alive.

Mentors Are Good Trainers

A good mentor is a trainer. He is not envious when he sees his people basking in fame and affluence because he is a people developer and a team builder. He can sense the talents hidden in the most unlikely people and transform them into responsible individuals. He harnesses and organizes his mentees' strengths to maximize their productivity. He mobilizes, inspires, develops and empowers them for a common goal. He wastes no time complaining about how bad the people under him are, but spends his time considering and developing strategies on how to make those ordinary people great.

Human beings cannot train themselves to become their best in life. You do not have all that it takes to make yourself the best that you can be. Your destiny is tied to the loins of some other people on whose shoulders you can stand and see farther. You must understudy someone or be coached by someone else before you fulfill your destiny. No human being becomes their best in life without a mentor. If you are not a student of someone else, you cannot excel in your field and be able to coach someone else. Tutelage and apprenticeship are important in every field of life.

Mentorship is not about ambitions, titles or positions. Mentors do not coach people because they want to be known or popular. They develop others through their personal examples. Mentors model excellence as they help others maximize their potential and reach their destiny. They train them to be the best in their different callings, they sharpen their blunt edges and make them threshing instruments to defeat the powers of the enemy. They train and release. As others input into you, your worth increases. No man is an island.

No eaglet can become a full eagle without being taught by its mother to fly. Its wings are developed only in the skies as it flies. She carries the eaglet in the air and drops it occasionally to exercise its wings. It stays close to pick up the baby eagle when it is about to crash. There is no calling in life that several others have not walked in before you. They have gone before you and excelled in the field into which God is calling you. Tapping from the numerous graces upon their lives will help you avoid the mistakes they made, help you to do better and reach your destiny. They are your destiny helpers who will help you fulfill your vision in life and stretch you to pull out the best in you. You cannot see farther or excel without climbing up on their shoulders.

You must be a good disciple of someone else before you can become a good mentor to others. Anyone who is not a follower is not worthy to be followed. There are two important groups of people in your life: those you follow and look up to, whose graces you desire to tap into to fulfill your destiny; and those who follow your footsteps and are gleaning from the graces you carry, looking to fulfill their own destinies. If you locate your mentor, make a conscious effort to inform and remind him from time to time that you are relying on him for mentorship.

Mentors Are Ladders for Their Mentees to Climb

Many people are continually moving around the same areas of their lives and cannot make progress because they do not have mentors. Dr. David Oyedepo of Living Faith Ministries worldwide, says "without fathers, you have no feathers and without feathers, you cannot fly."

Those who jumped to the top without climbing a ladder easily crash from there. You need a ladder to get to the top. Your mentor or spiritual father is the ladder you climb to get to the top. Many have disregarded the ladder provided for them and have wrecked their lives, marriages, and ministries in the process. They try to make it through every crooked means available to them but end up failing to reach their destinies. If you neglect your ladder to the top, you will struggle and never get there.

The quality of your mentor determines how far you can go in life. They can only give to you what they have. Prayerfully choose your mentor. It should be someone whose grace and anointing you desire and yearn for. Look for someone whose lifestyle you wish to emulate.

We need both spiritual and career mentorship. You are free to have as many mentors and fathers as possible depending on your different mandates in life and their areas of specialization.

Mentors Pull Out the Potential In Us.

We all are loaded with potential to become stars in our various fields. No one is a nonentity, and no one is useless in God's vineyard. Unfortunately, some live and die without displaying their potential or being able to use it to impact their world. Wise coaches and mentors know how to draw out our potential and ensure that we use them to bless our world.

Your leadership potential can only be drawn out by others who believe in you and are willing to strengthen you. Mentorship is God's system for maximizing your potential.

Mentors Teach Us Sacrificial Living.

No one ever makes it to the top without making sacrifices along the line. Any man whose life is a success story is diligent, Proverbs 22:29. A lazy man will never leave great footprints on the sands of time. It is impossible for lazy people to walk in the footsteps of giants. If you desire to reach the top, you must be ready to make some sacrifices to diligently catch up with those who've succeeded and are already on the frontline.

There are people in life who make history. But most people are spectators, reading the news others have made. Someone has said that the graveyard is the richest place on earth because of the wealth-producing ideas that people who did not deliver their mandates took to their graves. Sadly, they are useless in the grave. They are needed here where they will touch lives and impact generations.

Mentors Make You Relevant to Your World.

As other people add to your life, it increases your worth. None of us is an island. You only qualify to be referred to if you are referring to someone who has gone ahead of you. A single tree cannot make a forest. We all need the input and covering of others to become our best and be shielded from the scorching heat of the sun.

To read biographies of great men in your field is a great help. You get to know their strengths and weaknesses, their achievements and failures. That can help you avoid the mistakes they made in life. You are also able to set standards for yourself considering their accomplishments. Study them and see what principles you can adopt from them. Discover their development, stage-by-stage. Their stories are available everywhere, especially on the Internet. Even if you never meet them personally, you can be impacted through their teachings.

Your mentor can only give you what he has. The quality of your mentor, in large part, determines how far you can go in life. Choose your mentor prayerfully. Look for someone whose grace and anointing you would be happy to share, whose lifestyle you gladly emulate.

PRACTICAL EXAMPLES OF MENTORING IN THE BIBLE

Elijah and Elisha 2 Kings 3:11b

The relationship between Elijah and Elisha is a practical example of a mentor/mentee principle. Elisha served Elijah at close range till Elijah finished his ministry on earth. When he was getting close to the end of his ministry, while the other 50 sons of the prophets watched him from afar, Elisha crossed the Jordan river with him, intent on staying close to him until he was taken away to heaven. Elisha was intent on tapping the grace upon his mentor, Elijah's, life and at that, was not satisfied with the measure of anointing that Elijah had. He wanted a double portion of Elijah's anointing. With that, he went from being a servant to become a son.

What you receive from your mentor depends on the relationship that exists between the two of you and the kind of service you render to him. If you serve him for wages, you will receive your wages. But, if you serve as a son for an inheritance, then you will receive an inheritance.

When Elijah was being taken up into heaven, Elisha screamed "My father, my father, the chariot of Israel and its horsemen, what about the mantle?"

At that point when the relationship was clearly defined as a father-son relationship, Elijah released the mantle to him because, as a son, he was entitled to his father's inheritance, even if he did not work for it. As he took the mantle and put it on his shoulders, he received a double portion of the spirit of Elijah.

On his way back, he put his mantle on the water and it divided. When the other sons of the prophets saw it, they said the spirit of Elijah now rests on Elisha. (2 Kings 2:13–14)

Aquila And Priscilla Mentored Apollos

In Acts 18:24-28, we read how Priscilla and Aquila were used mightily of the Lord to mentor Apollos.

They heard him preach God's Word and discovered that Apollos was eloquent, and persuasive, but lacked knowledge because he only knew the baptism of John.

At this time, John had finished his ministry and had passed the baton to Jesus. Jesus had finished His and had handed it to the Holy Spirit. Apollos was two dispensations behind, still preaching John the Baptist in the era of the Holy Spirit!

They did not despise or write Apollos off. They saw that he could be a mighty vessel in God's hand, took him under their wings and taught him God's Word. They mentored him until he caught up, became relevant, and because of their mentoring grace, Apollos became one of the pillars of the early Church.

David Mentored Worthless Men

In 1 Samuel 22:2, we read that:

All those who were in distress or in debt or discontented, gathered around him, and he became their leader, about four hundred men were with him.

David saw himself as a transformational leader and a mentor. He did not go looking for those who were already made. He took the worst of men and transformed them into the greatest leaders of his time. He transformed a band of miscreants into one of the most effective and disciplined armies the world had ever known. They became known as "the mighty men of David." From distressed and discontented men to mighty men. What a glorious transformation!

Mentoring brings about this level of transformation. David was a great mentor, and the result manifested in the men he raised over time. We need mentors like David, who can make room for weaklings and trust God, in time, to turn them into warriors. He was a transformational leader indeed!

Transformational leaders empower others to fulfill the God's purpose for their lives. They help people discover and develop their gifts and use them in the Lord's service. They enable others to fulfill God's mandate on their lives. They focus on people, to develop their potentials and help them to become the best they can be. They do not use their leadership power to frustrate, intimidate, or alienate those who are opposed to some of their views or approaches. They use it to teach them to stir up their lives and to enable them to reach their destiny and maximize their potential. They use it to do good to others and bring healing to the hurting.

David created an enabling atmosphere that helped those worthless men to develop their potentials. He did not wield the power of life and death over them. He saw that his role was essentially as that of a good coach, pouring his life into them, and helping them develop their God-given potential.

Eunice And Louis Mentored Timothy in 2 Timothy 1:5-6

God used Eunice and Lois to disciple young Timothy as an spiritual son and mentee to the Apostle Paul. They were able to transfer their faith and relationship with God to him. (2 Timothy 1:5-6) Paul described Timothy as his best son in the faith because of the input of two apostolic women in Timothy's life and ministry.

Philip's Wife Mentored Her Four Daughters

Philip's wife was a great wife and leader, who took time to mentor her four virgin daughters as apostolic daughters, prophetesses, and virgins. (Acts 21:8-9) The society where they found themselves was not in any way better than ours. It was as hard then to live righteous lives as it is now. Yet, "Mrs. Philip" was able to mentor her four daughters, groom them so well that they grew up and kept their virginity and were also great vessels of honor in God's hands. We need to make time to mentor not only our biological children, but others God brings to us as well.

As an apostolic leader, make time to mentor people God brings to you. Train yourself to mentor and equip men and women, young and old, to flow in full apostolic authority, power, and grace.

Naomi and Ruth

Ruth was Naomi's widowed daughter-in-law. After Naomi lost her husband and two sons and was left with only her daughters-in-law, she encouraged them to go back to their people and remarry. Orpah left, but Ruth clung to her mother-in-law and refused to leave her. Naomi began to mentor Ruth until she married Boaz. Ruth was obedient to Naomi and carried out all the instructions she gave her.   Through Naomi's grooming, Ruth became hardworking and found favor in the sight of Boaz who later married her. Through mentoring, she and Naomi became great biblical examples of the kind of relationship that should exist between a mother- and daughter-in-law. When she had a child for Boaz, the women of the land said in Ruth 4:14-15:

> *And the women said unto Naomi, Blessed be the LORD, which hath not left thee this day without a kinsman, that his name may be famous in Israel. And he shall be unto thee a restorer of thy life, and a nourisher of thine old age: for thy daughter in law, which loveth thee, which is better to thee than seven sons, hath born him.*

Though she was a Moabitess; her name appears in the genealogy of Jesus Christ through mentoring.

Paul mentored Timothy.

Paul told Timothy in 2 Timothy 2:2,

And the things that thou hast heard of me among many witnesses, the same commit thou to faithful men, who shall be able to teach others also.

He poured himself into Timothy, his beloved son in the faith. No wonder he told him in 2 Timothy 1:13-14

Hold fast the pattern of sound words which you have heard from me, in faith and love which is in Christ Jesus. That good thing which was committed to you, keep by the Holy Spirit who dwells within you.

He also told him in 2 Timothy 3:10, 14:

...but you have carefully followed my doctrine, manner of life, purpose, faith, longsuffering, love, perseverance, persecutions, afflictions.... but you must continue in the things which you have learned and been assured of, knowing from whom you have learned them.

The apostles of old were more interested in building men than structures because they had the highest regard for mentoring, which has to do with teaching, instructing and influencing someone else. It influences the way you think and behave and imparts to others the principles that govern your life. Mentoring makes a difference in anyone's life. It is a blessing to recognize your mentor and instructor when you meet him. He may be your contemporary or an old friend, who may be younger or older than you. What matters is that you know he has what it takes for you to move to the next level of your life.

You may need to deal with pride and ego to submit to essential training. You may also need to release some preconceived notions that may have shaped your thinking about promotion processes in life. For you to experience radical breakthroughs in life, God may need to radically refresh you.

Paul's greatest joy emanated from seeing other ministers excel, even better than himself, and finally becoming who God wanted them to be. That was his motivation and drive. He desired to bless others and sought ways to transform even seemingly worthless leaders into great ones that gladdened God's heart. He did not entice people with material things to belong to his apostolic network. People joined because they were hungry for spiritual gain.

Chapter Eight

THE CHALLENGES OF LEADERSHIP

Leaders are not exempt from the storms of life. From time to time, you will meet storms and tempests on your voyage through life. Don't run back to port because of it. You are to battle through the life's storms without fear. Whether we travel by air, land or sea, bumps are inevitable.

A good pilot doesn't turn back from his journey or land in a hurry when he encounters a storm. All he does is tighten his seat belt and inform everyone aboard to tighten theirs and prepare to weather the storms. Remember that Jesus is the Captain of our boat and once He is there, our boat can never capsize no matter how turbulent the waves. The raging will not last forever. Be calm, stand still and see God's salvation.

Too Busy with Activities

A leader's schedule is often crowded with activities. If he is not careful, he'll become a busybody in other people's matters while his God-given assignment suffers. He needs to order his priorities to do what must be done, instead of attempting to please everyone at the expense of his relationship with God.

Our effectiveness and our spiritual worth stem from the time we spend with God. It is impossible to be a man of the people and be a man of God. Those who desire to always be with people and have no time for God have nothing to offer the people and will end up losing them. But when you make it your priority to spend time with God, in your quiet time with Him you'll receive the solutions to the needs of the people. God will direct you. When you spend time in His presence, you will learn to exchange what you have for what He has.

Elizabeth George in her book *A Woman After God's Heart* calls it "the great exchange." She said,

> "Away from the world and hidden from public view, I exchange my darkness for His light, my weakness for His power, my weariness for His strength, my problems for His solutions, my turmoil for his calm, my burdens for his freedom, my frustrations for His peace, my hopes for His promises, my afflictions for His balm of comfort, my questions for His answers, my confusion for his knowledge, my doubt for His assurance, my nothingness for His awesomeness, the temporal for the eternal, and the impossible for the possible."

Because of the things that compete for the 24 hours in our days, we may wish we had more of them. Of course, we know that God demands our ultimate attention. Our families are also there making their demands. Ministry activities and expectations also stare us in the face. How do we handle all these without anyone suffering?

Often the pressures that come from the ministry are so much that God is not given the priority He deserves, and our families also suffer. Granted, we do ministry work for the Lord, but it is one thing to work for Him and yet another thing to work with Him. He is more interested in those who work with Him than those who work for Him. Just an hour spent with the Lord each day can save you hours of frustration.

Discouragement and Weariness of heart

As leaders, there are times when we grow weary in well doing because we are not seeing quick answers to our prayers. We can also become discouraged when we see God's Word being fulfilled in the lives of people we have prayed for, and changes in their situations, but not our own.

Discouragement comes as an attack from the devil to weary us and cause us to question the integrity of God's Word in our lives. At times, God seems distant, and we can feel as if we're going in the opposite direction of our dreams or what God's promised us. It is needful at such times to put on strength and encourage ourselves in the Lord.

Use warfare Scriptures to deal with the Jezebel-type forces responsible for your discouragement and return their arrows back to them. Refuse to dialogue with the devil; he will have nothing good to offer. He has been a liar from the beginning, and no truth is found in him. Resist him and he will flee from you.

Have confidence in God. If He does not make a way for us, no man can. When we receive His approval, He supplies everything we need to forge ahead. It is important not to grow weary and give up, but to wait for Him. He does not lie. Part of what we need to get ourselves back to our feet when we are discouraged is to prophetically drain out of our lives every bit of stale oil and ask God to refill us with fresh anointing from on high. We also need to dust the ash of spiritual warfare off ourselves, change our stained garments in the spirit and re-arm ourselves for the next attack with our weapons of warfare, the cloak of humility, strength, and righteousness. Our fire needs to be rekindled so that the heat will melt away everything that would bind us. It also helps to rededicate ourselves to the Lord as living sacrifices.

If, as a leader, you look around and do not see tangible signs of God's goodness in your life and evidence that He is a rewarder of those who faithfully serve Him, it can be discouraging. We do not necessarily have to look at physical blessings, though they are important. You cannot quantify the value of souls snatched from hell because of your leadership.

God knows our personal needs and challenges, as well as our desires. He is an "on-time God," never early, nor is He ever late. We must remember that He never fails, neither does He promise to do what He cannot do. Don't allow your yet-to-be-answered prayers to distract or hinder your relationship with Him. We need to know that His global agenda is more important than our personal problems. If we will lay down our lives to meet those needs, He will surely meet ours.

We must courageously move knowing that those personal needs have been settled by the Lord in the spirit. At His own time, He will make them manifest. Just keep calling them forth with assurance that they have already been taken care of. He usually shows up when we least expect it.

Lack of Knowledge

Knowledge is power: They who know the name of their God will put their trust in Him. Many times, we lack content as leaders. If we have nothing inside of us, we have nothing to offer our world. Leadership is more effective if we have adequate knowledge of the right word that is needed by those to whom we minister. God clearly states in Hosea 4:6, *"My people perish for lack of knowledge."* There are appropriate Scriptures for every problem we have ever had or will ever have.

Certain sicknesses appear incurable and difficult to handle just because the right diagnosis has not been made and the right drug administered. In the same vein, problems and challenges seem insurmountable until the Lord gives us the right key or strategy to deal with them in prayer. Some of the prayers we pray are like shooting and missing the target. This is the season for precise praying that hits the target. We cannot afford to waste time and "ammunition." We need a clear understanding of the battle on the ground, receive from the Holy Spirit the right strategy for the battle, and apply it at the right time to get the desired result.

Some leaders are so religious they are of little earthly use. They consider it a sin to be aware of, or in touch with happenings around them. They do not read the newspapers or listen to the broadcast news. How can they pray effectively without adequate knowledge of what is happening around them?

Admittedly, the Holy Spirit sometimes prays through us and takes care of issues that we do not even know about, but it is still important to have accurate knowledge of the things happening around you, so we can pray correctly. If we are to be effective watchmen over the affairs of the global Church and the nations of the world, we cannot be like Israel's watchmen described in Isaiah 56:10:

His watchmen are blind: they are all ignorant, they are all dumb dogs, they cannot bark; sleeping, lying down, loving to slumber.

We can't afford to be blind and ignorant of what is happening around us else we will be like the proverbial ostrich that buries its head in the sand. Its body is fully exposed to danger yet presumes all is well (Job 39:13-17).

Daniel and his colleagues were governmental leaders in the government of Babylonian King Nebuchadnezzar. They were described in Daniel 1:4 as…

Young men, in whom there is no blemish, but good-looking, gifted in all wisdom, possessing knowledge, and quick to understand, who could serve in the king's palace, and whom they might teach the language and literature of the Chaldeans.

So, they were intelligent, versatile, knowledgeable and willing to learn new things.

Lack of Openness and Transparency

It takes humility to be transparent in our dealings with God, and others. Your pride will occasionally fight against your being open and transparent. It will cause you to bottle up things you ought to share openly. God wants you to speak the truth from your heart. You can hide nothing from Him. He sees your hearts.

If your character is intact, no matter what you lose, your destiny is still intact. If the devil cannot touch your character, he cannot touch your destiny. Character is your distinctive identity. It is what you are known for. It is your attitude and action in secret, who you are when no one is watching. Character is your behavior under pressure. Real character is revealed in adversity.

Under normal circumstances, everybody behaves normally. But when a man is under pressure, the content of who he truly is surfaces. The real strength of a man is his strength of character. The strength of your character determines the strength of your destiny. You cannot have a destiny bigger and higher than your character. It is impossible for one to have weak character and end with a strong destiny. You are doing nothing about your destiny until you are doing something about your character.

Our transparency, especially in confessing our faults to others, encourages them to know that they are not alone in their struggles. It gives them hope and helps them not to give up. Proverbs 28:13 tells us that:

He that covers his sins shall not prosper: but whoso confesses and forsakes them shall have mercy.

When we take off our masks and come to the Lord the way we are, He can reveal His agenda to us. He sees our weaknesses and is willing to deal with them when we stop pretending that they do not exist. Our transparency also enables other Christians to pray for us more specifically and strategically since they understand our frailties and challenges.

Lack Of Provisions For The Work

Scripture reminds us that money answers all things. Money is a servant and a major tool that we need to carry out our assignments. It is as important in this work as are the human resources. It should not in any way hinder us from carrying out the special assignments given to us by the Lord.

Since He is the one who deploys us to various fields, He assumes responsibility to pay the bills. He can provide all that is needed for His work to be carried out. He wants us to trust and believe Him for every provision and to walk with Him by faith. He is the one who anoints our hands to make wealth. He encourages us to always apply to the Supplier whenever we run out of supplies.

Disillusionment

Disillusionment is one of the weapons the devil employs in spiritual warfare. Most times, after leaders have done great exploits for the Lord, they are hit with a wave of disillusionment. They begin to see themselves like Elijah after his victory on Mount Carmel. Discouragement and depression comes over them and makes them want to give up their faith, courage, and enthusiasm for God. They feel like they have taken in so much, they cannot handle any more pressure.

Satan specializes in attacking us in our greatest strength with the intentions to weaken and discourage us. He comes with fear and intimidation to steal God's plans and gifts from us and tries to make us believe that we cannot take any more. We begin to grumble against God and tell Him that we have reached our limit and cannot cope beyond that level.

Elijah was so discouraged and depressed that he gave up on life and, in his despair, desired to go home to glory and rest. He began to grumble and complain to God that they have killed His prophets and he was the only one left. But God said to him that he still had over 7,000 prophets who had not yet bowed their knees to Baal. God did not stop him from His desire to come home. Note: Elijah did not go home because he had finished his assignment. He went home because he desired to go home.

Out of disillusionment, instead of asking God for the grace and strength to continue because of all his challenges, he asked to go home. God has an agenda for us all. We can only get the best from our Christian lives when we follow His timetable. He has the manual for successful living. When we attempt to run our lives ourselves and make major decisions out of disillusionment, we run into danger.

Disillusionment will keep you from seeking God and cause you to bury yourself in other activities that have no eternal value. These activities distract you from the real thing and give you a false sense of satisfaction. You see yourself withdrawing and hiding from God like Adam did. Disillusionment makes you restless and unsettled both in your walk with God and in working for Him. You cannot afford to become passive and withdraw from God and His agenda because of disillusionment.

When you are disillusioned, you can sometimes busy yourself with religious activities and drift from church to church because you do not believe the churches are spiritual enough to meet your needs. You get possessed by the spirit of religion and are not able to know the mind of God for your life. You may have been faithful to God all your life, but just on the verge of your breakthrough; you are swept off your feet and unable to see the end of God's plan for your life.

Throwing a spiritual tantrum does not force God to respond earlier to your case than He would have otherwise. It only makes it impossible for you to surrender to His will for your life. You do not need to know the end from the beginning before you can trust God.

Disillusionment blocks God from considering your case and hinders His restorative healing power from being released into your situation. Do not forget that Satan is a great opportunist. He attacks when you are down and discouraged. Those are his best times to encounter you. He will use every chance he gets to accomplish his schemes against you.

We sometimes find it difficult to handle the aftermaths of spiritual warfare or shattered dreams. My greatest consolation is that God is the repairer of the broken walls and shattered lives. No matter how battered we are, God specializes in repairing our brokenness. He is not interested in seeing us merely exist, barely managing to breathe. He came that we might have life and have it more abundantly. (John 10:10)

One major antidote for disillusionment is for us to remember the goodness and mercies of God and to praise Him in the midst of life's challenges. Allow God's mercies and love to saturate your soul and His peace that passes all understanding to envelop your heart. Praise keeps you above your circumstances.

Sometimes God allows situations in our lives to not only teach us His sovereignty, but also to draw us closer to Him. When we are faced with challenges, He becomes even more real to us. If we learn to hang onto Him, aware that He is with us through the floods and in the fire to ensure that no harm befalls us, we will emerge from our trials victorious. (Isaiah 43:2-3)

Another of God's reasons for allowing such situations in our lives is to bring us to a point of knowing Him personally, not just believing what other people have said about Him. God knows our strengths and abilities better than we do. He does not allow us to bite off more than He knows we can chew. In 2 Corinthians 1:3-4 Paul said:

> *Praise be to the God and Father of our Lord Jesus Christ, the Father of compassion and the God of all comfort, who comforts us in all our troubles, so that we can comfort those in any trouble with the comfort we ourselves have received from God.*

And in 1 Corinthians 10:13 he said:

> *No temptation has seized you except what is common to man. And God is faithful; He will not let you be tempted beyond what you can bear. But when you are tempted, He will also provide a way out so that we can stand up under it.*

If all were easy where would the cross be, where would we fight? But in the hard place, God proves what He can do. Be not disillusioned regardless of what you are going through. There is a word of encouragement in Isaiah 41:10:

> *So do not fear, for I am with you; do not be dismayed, for I am your God. I will strengthen you and help you; I will uphold you with my righteous right hand.*

Once Jesus is in your boat, you can smile at the storms. God does not allow us to go through any form of physical or emotional pain just for the fun of it. He trains us through those things, so we can help others who pass through similar situations.

Every useful enterprise demands sacrifice. A worthy price must be paid to get a worthwhile result in all our endeavors.

Loneliness

It can be quite lonely at the top at times. You are a servant of the people, as well as their coach and role model. They look up to you and want to be like you. That puts you in a unique situation. As their servant, you may lose some of your freedom to be yourself. You may, at times, be a bit isolated from them. Sometimes, those who follow you will keep their distance, as a sign of respect. Most of the time, however, people will bring you their problems looking for solutions.

Lack of Vision

Vision is the power of imagination. It is your ability to see the destination before the journey begins. Leaders see what others cannot see because they see it with the eyes of the spirit. They see themselves already becoming what they see in the future. Vision comes with foresight. You see the finished product of what you are about to produce with the eyes of faith. Your vision is the reason for your existence, what you are living for. It is that which you want to accomplish for God as your contribution to your generation. Your vision keeps you going and becomes your driving force.

The more you see it in your spirit, the more energized you will be to pursue it. You will gladly give up anything in pursuit of the vision. It provides you with direction and purpose for living and will keep you from discouragement and distraction.

Your vision is the driving force that keeps you going and helps you to accomplish uncommon feats in your generation. As leader, you must be able to communicate your vision to your followers and convince them to take ownership. It is to become their vision as well. If you cannot sell your vision to people and carry them along to achieve it, you either do not have one or do not understand it.

How far you can see into the future will affect and determine who you are today. No wonder, *"Where there is no vision, the people perish"* (Proverbs 29:18). Different people, looking at the same thing, can see it differently. Apostolic leaders see ahead. They know what it will take to get there and can carry other people along to that destination. They do not succumb to the status quo or flow with the system. They not only read the news of what others are doing, they create their own news. They are the pacesetters, pioneers who blaze the trail for others to follow.

Your vision drives you and gives you your mission. As you embark on your mission, your vision will be accomplished. Choose a project you can embark on to help you carry out your vision. Actualizing it gets you to the cutting edge of life. At that level, life becomes exciting because you can see your impact on your world. People want solutions, not problems. They want answers to the numerous questions in their hearts. They want assets, not liabilities. We need to make a positive impact that counts.

No matter how wonderful your vision is, if you lack the discipline to pursue it to completion, it remains dormant till you die. Habakkuk 2:2 states the need to…

Write the vision and make it plain on tables, that he may run who reads it. For the vision is yet for an appointed time, but at the end, it will speak, and it will not lie, though it tarries, wait for it, because it will surely come, it will not tarry.

Many have a God-given vision, but never received instructions on how they were to achieve it. They died without their visions becoming reality. It takes a missionary to receive a vision, cast it to the people in such a way that they take ownership and help complete it.

You cannot run with a vision you do not understand. You cannot see what is ahead of you except the eyes of your heart are open. No wonder Paul prayed this powerful prayer for the Ephesian Christians in Ephesians 1:18:

That the eyes of your understanding will be enlightened, that you may know what is the hope of your calling, what are the riches of the glory of his inheritance in the saints.

Many Christians see physically, but their spiritual eyes are shut. David prayed for himself in Psalm 13:3 saying; *"Consider and hear me, O Lord my God, enlighten my eyes, lest I sleep the sleep of death."*

Spiritual Emptiness

No believer can survive and be effective without adequate knowledge of the Word. God's Word is creative, sharp, effective and powerful. It is life. It is our mirror. It sharpens and builds us up. All that we need to prosper in life is found in the Word.

Cultivate a habit of spending time studying and meditating on the Word of God, not just once in a long while but every day. (2 Timothy 2:15) Some pastors read or study the Bible only to prepare their messages, not to feed their spirit man. It is the Word of God that fuels our prayer lives. Meditate on it until it becomes revelation from the Holy Spirit, richly dwelling in our heart. (Colossians 3:16) When you speak from your mouth and meditate on it in your heart, it will make you prosperous and give you good success. (Joshua 1:8)

We are all busy, but amid your tight schedule, set aside time to study God's Word and to read other good books and materials that will give you the knowledge you need for success. Read, study and listen to the bible and to good Christian messages on CDs, iPods, and iPad. Set aside quality time to enrich yourself. Second Timothy 2:15 encourages us to study to show ourselves approved unto God, a workman that needs not to be ashamed, rightly dividing the word of truth.

Apostolic leaders sometimes load themselves with lots of activities that sap them of their energy. So much stress is experienced by the body in the process coupled with days of fasting. They are exhausted and not given any opportunity to rest. Many of them have no time to eat good food, exercise their bodies, have fun and just enjoy their lives. They see the Christian life as all about working and laboring for Christ.

Sometimes we get so busy working in another man's vineyard and receiving no reward for our labor, that we overlook our routine medical checkups. Some of us have serious health challenges like high blood pressure, diabetes and other chronic diseases. But some of us are either unaware of it, or do not tend to it until it is out of hand. Many are so engrossed with ministry and trying to meet the needs of the whole world that they neglect their families. Their spouses and children are groaning in pain because they are not there for them. They are too busy doing ministry.

Unconfessed Sin

God knows we are not yet perfect. As much as He desires that we live a holy life since we are clothed in His righteousness, He also knows that we will make mistakes. That is why He stated clearly in 1 John 2:1-2:

My little children, these things write I unto you, that ye sin not. And if any man sin, we have an advocate with the Father, Jesus Christ the righteous: And he is the propitiation for our sins: and not for ours only, but also for the sins of the whole world.

When we are convicted of sin, by the Holy Spirit, the best thing we can do is to confess it from our heart, receive forgiveness, and move forward. David said in Psalms 66:18: *"If I regard iniquity in my heart, the Lord will not hear me."*

And in Proverbs 28:13, Solomon said,

He that covers his sins shall not prosper: but whoso confesses and forsakes them shall have mercy.

If we consciously tolerate sin in our lives, our ministries will be ineffective. Though we cannot hide our sins from God, He takes delight in our coming to Him with broken and contrite hearts to confess them. When we confess our sins to God, He forgives us, throws our sins into His Sea of forgetfulness and remembers them no more. (Jeremiah 31:34)

When God forgives and forgets our sins, our records are clean. It is our responsibility to receive His forgiveness and not allow the devil to trouble our hearts with false guilt. Many believers struggle in this area. They confess their sins to God. He forgives them, but they do not know how to forgive themselves and move forward. They keep running around the circle of regret, self-pity, false guilt, and unforgiveness.

There is a significant difference between conviction and condemnation. Every voice of condemnation comes from the devil.

God's forgiveness wipes out our sin, though not necessarily the consequences of our sin. Sin creates enmity between God and us. It keeps us from fellowship with Him. It could make us insensitive to God's voice or even dull our hearing. It keeps us running from God instead of running to Him. Isaiah 59:1-2 explains it better;

> *Behold, the Lord's hand is not shortened, that it cannot save; neither his ear heavy, that it cannot hear. But your iniquities have separated you from your God. And your sins have hidden His face from you, so that He will not hear.*

Sin can affect our relationships with other people. The devil tells us that everyone around us knows what we have done and are talking about us. Sin can destroy our lives and destinies if we practice it habitually. When you have laid your sin on His altar, hand have received His forgiveness, move forward.

Expect the enemy to harass you with false guilt, after you have confessed your sins to God. He enjoys overwhelming us with false guilt, self-pity, and condemnation. However, Romans 8:1 says: *There is therefore now no condemnation to them which are in Christ Jesus, who walk not after the flesh, but after the Spirit.*

Inadequate Training

Do not assume that you know everything you need to know. Learn new things every day to become proficient in your assignment. Unwillingness to learn to become better in your field limits you from getting to your ultimate in God. Learning is the quickest way to grow. It is preparing yourself for your future. You must keep learning if you desire to remain on the frontline as a leader, for when you stop learning you stop growing and stop leading. You learn your way up the ladder of success.

Your choice of materials to learn from is entirely your responsibility. You cannot afford to read all the material you see, listen to everything you hear, obey every instruction you receive, or develop a meaningful relationship with everyone you meet. You must choose your materials and your teachers.

In learning, you are to achieve sufficient knowledge to catapult you to your destiny. Do what you must do to increase your knowledge, value, and worth so that you can put a worthy price tag on yourself. Read good materials and listen to good messages. Daniel read the books in Daniel 9:29 and understood that their captivity in Babylon was over. Be versatile. Read widely and wisely.

Training is useful for the following reasons:

- It helps you to receive the professional information you need to excel in your field.
- It sharpens, refines, and adds value to you.
- It equips you with skills, empowers you with the ability to process information, and enlarges the capacity of your brain to store more.
- Training gives you free publicity, favor, and recognition beyond your peers. You can be a success all round by undergoing good training.
- Training makes you courageous. Most of our fears are the result of inadequate training and lack of preparation.

If we will submit to training and prepare to face our fears with God on our side, we are sure to be victorious.

Operating Without A Mentor Or Prophetic Covering

An inability to locate and submit to your prophetic covering can curtail your destiny. Joshua was very successful in life and ministry because Moses, God's servant, who laid hands on and mentored him. (Deuteronomy 34:9)

Samson had already messed up his life, but God connected him with a lad who led him to the pillar which he held and was able to fulfill his destiny. We need to locate our destiny pillars, those upon whose shoulders we can stand.

We need to locate our destiny lampstands on which we can stand and shine. Nothing can boost a destiny better than standing on the wisdom, knowledge, and experience of wise, anointed and successful people who have gone ahead of us.

Your light need not remain under the bushel for life. You need to be put on the lampstand, so you can shine out to your world. You are too anointed to be ignored. God saved you and has deposited much in you to impact your world. You must shine forth. You have been hidden and ordinary far too long. Rise and shine, this is your finest hour. Locate a mentor who can help you excel in life and reach your destiny.

There are some levels in life and ministry that you can never get to by your own strength. Depend on God's grace of God in your life and the life of your mentor or covering. The grace under which you operate matters a lot in the things of the spirit. Who is your spiritual covering? On whose spiritual shoulders are you standing? Jesus excelled as a leader because He was full of grace. Luke 2:40 says:

And the child grew and became strong; he was filled with wisdom, and the grace of God was upon him.

He has released His fullness to all who will excel as leaders; grace for grace (John 1:16). The apostles excelled as leaders because great grace was upon them. Acts 4:33 confirms this:

> *With great power, the apostles continued to testify to the resurrection of the Lord Jesus, and much grace was upon them all.*

Bad Company

The company you keep shapes your habits, behaviors, speech, likes, dislikes, and lifestyle. It can attract life or death to you. It can attract failure and success to you. It can either add or subtract virtue to your life. Hang out with the right people who are heading the right direction.

The company you keep, to a large extent, determines how far you can go in life and ministry.

- *Iron sharpens iron, so a man sharpens the countenance of his friend.* (Proverbs 27:17)
- *He who walks with wise men will be wise, but the companion of fools will be destroyed.* (Proverbs 13:20)
- *Whoever keeps the law is a wise son. But a companion of gluttons shames his father.* (Proverbs 28:7)
- *Whoever loves wisdom makes his father rejoice but a companion of harlots wastes his wealth.* (Proverbs 29:3-5)
- *evil communication corrupts good manners.* (1 Corinthians 15:33)

If you partner with excellent people, you will learn their ways and tilt toward excellence. David said of himself in Psalms 119:63, *"I am a companion of all who fear you and of all who keep your precepts."* No wonder he is called the man after God's heart.

Watch the company you keep. Great minds discuss ideas, ordinary minds discuss events, and lesser minds discuss people. Who are the friends that you hang out with? Sampson's life and destiny were cut short because of his wrong association with Delilah. The many rebels that followed Absalom died the day he died because of association.

It is safer to stand alone than to hang out with the wrong people. Anyone who does not share your convictions about God and life will not likely be heading toward your destination. Hold on to your innocence and good character instead of allowing bad friends to corrupt you. Look for friends who will increase your value and make you a better and more influential Christian. Good friends help you to think your best thoughts, do your noblest deeds, pursue your best dreams, and be your finest self.

Life is made up of three groups of people, those who pull you down to their level, those who pull you alongside with them and those who pull you up to where they are. Your primary associations should be with people who pull you along and up to your finest self, those who fan the flame of your life to a point that you become passionate for God. True friends will encourage you through thick and thin.

When you hang out with the wrong people, they poison your spirit man with junk and pollution that keeps you at the level of continual repentance and dries the flow of your spiritual life. The right company will sharpen you, strengthen your prayer life, and help you to stay focused to fulfill your destiny. There are friends who are meant for a certain season and then gone when the season is over, allowing you to move forward. If you try to carry them into the pages and chapters of your life where they do not belong, they become excess luggage and hinder you from making meaningful progress. Some phone numbers will need to be deleted from your phone if you are to move forward in life.

Inability to Take Risks or Handle Life's Challenges

On your journey through life, you will always meet the discouragers, the pessimists, the mockers and the doubters. Because they do not see beyond their noses, they make you think that no one can ever be a good leader. Look beyond the obstacles they place in your path and forge ahead.

Winners never quit, and quitters never win. Don't be afraid to fail. If you try and fail, try, try again. You do not know what you can do until you make the effort to do it.

Lack of Discipline

Discipline is an orderly or prescribed conduct or pattern of behavior that corrects, molds, or perfects one's mental ability or moral character.

Give yourself some deadlines to accomplish your goals. Decide which extra effort you need to make to accomplish your dreams. It will cost you something. Cultivate the skills and behavior you need to get to your destination, e.g., a pleasant disposition, a positive walk with people, hard work, a winning smile, etc. Do your best to work on your weaknesses.

Discipline yourself to write down your goals and how long it should take you to achieve them. However, deserving of praise or commendation your vision is, it is only wishful thinking if it is not actualized and brought to reality. Henry Kaiser said,

> "Determine what you want more than anything else in life, write down how you intend to attain it, and permit nothing to deter you from pursuing it."

Bill Newman said,

"Without goals and priorities, we will never escape the tyranny of the urgent. If we do not have our eyes fixed on the goal, the urgent will crowd the important."

Poor Time Management

Apostolic leaders are efficient time managers. You only have 24 hours a day. Many people and activities compete for those 24 hours. Discipline yourself to prioritize your time, so worthwhile and fruitful things take the bulk of your day. Share your time in a way that God and your family get your best attention. Make room for friends who add value to your life and pull you up to a higher level in your walk with God. Choose activities that lead you into a deeper walk with God, activities that will instill in you the spirit of excellence like studying God's Word, praying, reading useful materials, etc.

Limit interaction with friends and activities that deter you from your life vision. They must not be allowed to eat away your precious time. Avoid fruitless gossip about people. Prioritize your life and eliminate non-essentials. Do not allow other peoples' lack of planning to constitute constant emergencies for you. Keep to schedules and deadlines. Time is to guide you. Do not abuse it or become a slave to it. Learn to delegate certain responsibilities without abdicating.

Disobedience to God's Word

God's Word is all we need to live our lives to please him. It is our manual, and in it is everything necessary for us to become or to get what we need in life. We need it to fulfill our destiny. It is the most important book of the ages, containing stories of great leaders and the secrets behind their success. Everything required to be an effective apostolic leader is found inside.

We attract lots of benefits to our lives when we obey the instructions written in it. According to Proverbs 3:2, it adds long life and peace to us. In Proverbs 4:22, it is life to those who find it and health to all their flesh. God's words can keep us safe from harm when we store them in our hearts. Proverbs 6:21-22 confirms this:

Bind them continually upon your heart and tie them about thy neck. When you go, it shall lead you; when thou sleep, it shall keep you; and when you awake, it shall talk with you.

No one can live a meaningful life in this world without obeying God's Word. Proverbs 7:1-3 tells of its importance:

My son, keep my words, and lay up my commandments with you, keep my commandments and live; and my law as the apple of your eye. Bind them upon your fingers, write them upon the table of your heart."

To refuse to obey God's Word will diminish your influence and impact, as well as possibly endanger your life and destiny. (Proverbs 5:13-14) If we practice what is written in it as we are encouraged to do in Joshua 1:8, we will make our ways prosperous and have good success. The easiest way of doing God's work is to receive specific instruction from Him and obey it implicitly. Obedience will save us from a lot of headaches, shield us from the arrows of the enemy, and deliver us from making costly mistakes. Like Samuel told Saul in 1 Samuel 15:22-23:

Behold, to obey is better than sacrifice, and to hearken than the fat of rams. For rebellion is as the sin of witchcraft, and stubbornness is as iniquity and idolatry.

The best way to exhibit our faith in God is by obeying Him. Even if His instructions do not make sense to our human minds, it pays to obey Him. He is the one who knows the end from the beginning. He knows the way through the wilderness. The best we can do is to trust and obey. As the old hymn says, "There is no other way to be happy in Jesus, but to trust and obey." Going where He sends us and doing what He instructs us to do is how we reach our destiny.

God cannot contradict Himself. We cannot afford to come boldly before God's throne of grace to present our petitions when we are disobedient. (2 Corinthians 10:6) We cannot blatantly disobey Him and expect Him to answer our prayers. Our obedience can give us miracles and breakthroughs that we would otherwise have not receive. It pays to obey God implicitly. Partial obedience is as bad as outright disobedience. It is better to obey God rather than man. Even if God instructions seem difficult, once we are willing to obey Him, He makes it easy for us.

Disobedience is rebellion, which is an antichrist spirit. Obeying God is unconditional. It is not done because you need a breakthrough from God or you need your problems solved. We obey God because we love Him. Obedience is doing what we're told with a good heart attitude. It should be a lifestyle.

In John 13:35 Jesus says to us: *"if you love Me, keep My commandment."* Our love for Him is the basis for our obedience. Obedience stems from the heart. It is the easiest and fastest way of doing God's work and working with Him. A life of obedience will take you to heights nothing else will. The first order in heaven is obedience. Disobedience questions His authority, rebels against His government, and keeps us far from Him.

Unforgiveness

Many great men and women of God who should have been movers and shakers in the Kingdom have ended up becoming complainers because they embraced unforgiveness and bitterness. Unforgiveness and bitterness wrap around the neck of your destiny and potential and choke the life out of them. They leave the door open to the enemy.

Famed author and pastor, T.D. Jakes has said:

Unforgiveness is almost an epidemic. It is a mechanism of hell. It can incapacitate your whole body by just holding down one part of your life.

This cancer eats up pastors, prophets, intercessors, and their spouses. It has broken many relationships, ended many marriages, and destroyed many ministries whose futures looked so bright. It is a strong chain that is not easily broken. We are enjoined in Ephesians 4: 32 to:

...Be kind and compassionate to one another, forgiving each other, just as God in Christ forgave you.

Unforgiveness keeps you at the mercy of the person who keeps offending you and withholds your own forgiveness from God. He gave us a very clear injunction in Matthew 6:14 that,

If ye forgive men their trespasses, your heavenly Father will also forgive you; but if ye forgive not men their trespasses, neither will your heavenly father forgive your trespasses.

In spiritual warfare, unforgiveness leaves a hole in your armor, which the enemy can exploit to accuse, torment and give you sleepless nights.

Inability to Cope with Criticism and False Accusations.

It is mandatory that apostolic leaders learn to cope with criticism, knowing that no matter how good you are, you will be criticized. As a leader, understand that criticism is such a common thing that people are even criticized after they have died. People are different. Each has his own opinion about many things. It is liberating to live your life free from the opinions of others, or the need for their validation or approval. No matter how you try, you will never please everyone.

There will always be people who will analyze and find fault with everything you do. Pessimistic people only see the negative side of things. They hardly see anything good in what others do. We must constantly seek God's approval. It is very important as a leader to have a close walk with the Holy Spirit and be validated by Him. Living according to the opinions of men will not stand the test of time.

Even Jesus our example, God's sinless Son, was criticized and falsely accused. If they criticized him, they will also criticize you. He did not allow the opinions or criticism of men to distract Him from His purpose--His calling. Do not be unduly influenced by others or addicted to their approval because you lack self-confidence and are unable to make your own decisions and stand by them.

If people criticize you constructively and there is some truth in what they are saying, do not sweep it under the carpet. Consider it and allow the Holy Spirit to help you deal with the things you are being criticized of. *Open rebuke is better than secret love. Faithful are the wounds of a friend, but the kisses of an enemy are deceitful.* (Proverbs 27:5-6)

But if criticism is destructive and full of lies, aimed at ruining you, refuse to be distracted or discouraged by it. Forge ahead. Men throw stones only at fruitless trees. Someone said that gossip is the toll that merely adequate pay to excellent people. They are jealous because they cannot get to where you are. Also remember that it is your divine destiny that the devil is after. Stay focused and refused to be discouraged.

Slander, gossip, and bad rumors are only powerful because people can easily believe them. In fact, people find it easier to believe and spread bad news than good news. They readily and unquestionably believe the lie and yield themselves as instruments in the devil's hands to pull down ministers of the gospel. False news spreads like wildfire. It is easier to spread a lie than the truth.

Once false news is released about someone, especially a Christian leader, people rarely bother to get with God and find out the truth. Even if it is a set up from the pit of hell, they still fall for it because of spiritual insensitivity and immaturity. We Christians too often lie in wait against each other, looking out for one's downfall, rather than encouraging them to stand. We specialize in killing our wounded soldiers instead of recovering them and restoring them back to the faith.

The motive behind false accusations is envy and jealousy. The aim is to destroy. The shocking thing about false accusations is the expertise with which the lies are framed. If you are not in the Spirit, you can hardly tell that they are lies because they sound so true and are so logical.

It is equally alarming the extent that men can go to publish such lies. It is not surprising because even Jesus suffered the same. (Matthew 28:12-14) Men gathered together and donated huge sums of money to publish lies that Jesus did not rise from the dead. A servant cannot be greater than his master. If Jesus was maligned and His name messed up, we should not expect any better. But truth cannot be covered for too long. At the right time, it will speak.

Being Active in The Flesh

Flesh is the greatest enemy to victorious Christian living. Dying to one's flesh is required if he or she is to experience the resurrected life of Christ. We must, as Paul, die daily. (1 Corinthians 15:31) Oddly, brokenness settles a lot of your warfare. You are no longer a pawn in the hands of the enemy when you are broken. Rather, you become a terror to him. Your voice becomes recognized both in the Kingdom of God and to the kingdom of darkness. You become usable in God's hands and fruitful in every good work. Romans 8:13 confirms this:

> *For if you live according to the flesh, you will die, but if by the spirit you put to death the works of the flesh, you will live.*

Galatians 5:16 throws more light on it:

> *I say then: walk in the Spirit, and you shall not fulfill the lust of the flesh. For the flesh lusts against the Spirit, and the Spirit against the flesh.*

Romans 8:5-8 says it all:

> *For those who live according to the flesh set their minds on the things of the flesh, but those who live according to the Spirit, the things of the Spirit... So then, those who are in the flesh cannot please God.*

Ephesians 4:22-24 states how to die to your flesh:

> *That you put off, concerning your former conduct, the old man which grows corrupt according to the deceitful lusts, and be renewed in the spirit of your mind, and that you put on the new man which was created according to God, in true righteousness and holiness.*

Brokenness qualifies you to become a vessel of honor that will work *with* God rather than merely working *for* Him. It brings out the sweet fragrances in you that will make you a blessing to your world.

www.ingramcontent.com/pod-product-compliance
Lightning Source LLC
Chambersburg PA
CBHW070602010526
44118CB00012B/1422